secrets of
powerful women

secrets of
powerful
women

LEADING CHANGE FOR
A NEW GENERATION

FOREWORD BY
Andrea Wong

INTRODUCTION BY
Rosario Dawson

voice

Hyperion New York

Library of Congress Cataloging-in-Publication Data

Secrets of powerful women / foreword by Andrea Wong ; introduction
by Rosario Dawson. — 1st ed.
        p. cm.
    ISBN 978-1-4013-4111-4
    1. Leadership in women—United States.   2. Women—Political
activity—United States.   3. Women executives—United States.

    HQ1421.S43 2010
    305.42092'273—dc22

                                                    2009037396

Hyperion books are available for special promotions and premiums.
For details contact the HarperCollins Special Markets Department in
the New York office at 212-207-7528, fax 212-207-7222, or email
spsales@harpercollins.com.

Book design by Karen Minster

FIRST EDITION

10 9 8 7 6 5 4 3 2 1

The essays contained in this book have common threads that run throughout, not the least of which is the impact that women can have on the next generation. To all women who are imparting their own secrets to power to their granddaughters, daughters, nieces, and the many other girls they encounter, we salute you, and this book is dedicated to you. To my own nieces, Erin, Anna, Alexa, and Elianna, this book is dedicated to you as well.

I'd also like to dedicate this book to **The White House Project**, a nonprofit organization that works tirelessly and smartly to advance women in leadership—in their communities, in business, in government, and, hopefully one day, all the way to the White House.

—Andrea Wong

This is dedicated to my two favorite women, my mom, Isabel Celeste, and my grandmother Isabel "Mimá" II. It is your collective fierceness and perseverance that inspires me. Your love, support, sacrifice, guidance, humor, and larger-than-life spirit moves me. It is my life's challenge and my aspiration to emulate and honor your greatness. I love you both dearly.

—Rosario Isabel Dawson

CONTENTS

Andrea Wong, President and CEO of Lifetime Networks,
speaking at the 2008 DNC Women's Caucus in Denver, Colorado

Andrea Wong

There is something special that happens when you get a group of powerful women in a room . . . and shut the door.

If you've ever had that experience, you know what I am talking about. It's not always easy to explain, but it's a very real and palpable dynamic. There's a sense of camaraderie that comes from the deep level of understanding of the opportunities and challenges women share. For example, we've all thought about the if and when of having children and how that decision will impact our careers. We've all had a woman—a teacher, a boss, a mother—positively affect our lives and help us get to where we are today. But, to varying degrees, we've also all felt or witnessed the effects, directly or indirectly, of a legacy of women's inequality, whether on the playing field, in our schools and homes, or at our workplaces.

Some people dismiss this kind of gathering as a "sorority." But it's not frivolous, superficial, or even corny. And it's not a forum for male-bashing. It's simply a safe, comfortable environment in which profound truth-telling is possible. It's an atmosphere where secrets can be shared *and* honored.

That is exactly what happened during the 2008 Democratic and Republican conventions at Lifetime's Future Frontrunners Summit. In both Denver and St. Paul, the sites of the two conventions, Lifetime and its partners *CosmoGirl!* and the nonprofit Declare Yourself gathered a diverse roster of leading politicians, journalists, and advocates to speak to the sixteen high school and college students who were winners of our Future Frontrunners essay contest. The initiative was part of Lifetime's award-winning Every Woman Counts campaign to empower and inspire women and girls to make their voices heard in *every* hall of power.

Behind the closed doors of the two Future Frontrunners Summits, the most seasoned politicians of both parties let down their guards and shared intimate details of their professional and personal experiences with great candor, humor, and grace.

The Future Frontrunners Summit speakers—and now the contributors to this book—come from big cities and small towns, representing nearly twenty states across the country. They are Democrats, Republicans, and Independents; white, African-American, Latina, and Asian-American; Christian, Jewish, and Muslim; single, married, and divorced. Yet their life lessons and advice for leadership have much in common, including the importance of passion, mentors, organizing a community, and simply being your authentic self. And their secrets about power are . . . well, powerful.

Smile more: Martha Burk, the former head of the National Council of Women's Organizations and leader of the fight to allow women to join the Augusta National Golf Club, reveals, "If we're too assertive, we're characterized as 'bitchy' and 'castrating.' This doesn't mean we can't be assertive and push hard. We just have to smile more while we're doing it."

The power of the petition: As a third-grader in Ohio, Lisa Maatz of the American Association of University Women (AAUW) had her first lobbying experience fighting for doors on the stalls of the girls' bathroom. As she writes, "I had first asked [the principal] for doors all by myself and got nothing. In fact, I got worse than nothing—I got dismissed, even disrespected. But when I gave Mr. Ginke a petition signed by two hundred of my classmates, I had doors in a week."

We may not be brilliant at more than one thing at once: "I was a single parent who owned a business and served in public office. Some days I was a great mother. Some days I was a very savvy businesswoman, and some days I was a brilliant mayor. I can't remember a single day when I was all three at the same time," confesses Representative Kay Granger (R-TX), "[but] my sons can iron and cook. My daughter can fix anything."

Spice Girls, don't let the system change you: Representative Loretta Sanchez (D-CA) recounts, "When I first ran for the Congress, my husband and I had dinner with some consultants to discuss strategy. One topic I remember vividly was my image. They wanted to frump me up! Some people think I'm too sexy, too spicy, too open, and too direct. But that works for me. I say, choose to be who you are!"

Stay put: Carol Jenkins, longtime reporter and anchor and now head of the Women's Media Center, shares a letter from her very first news director: " 'It has come to our attention that you are attempting to organize the women in the newsroom. Please feel free to leave at any time.' Well, I stayed in the newsroom for over thirty years."

Yikes, the path to politics can be unconventional: After surviving uterine cancer and becoming an advocate for women's health, actress Fran Drescher found herself meeting with First Lady Laura Bush's staff. "I said, 'Lame duck, schmame duck—I need to share my message with women around the world!' Before I knew it I had been appointed a Public Diplomacy Envoy by the U.S. State Department."

How to get things done: Representative Marsha Blackburn (R-TN) shares her favorite quote from Margaret Thatcher: "If you want something said, ask a man. If you want something done, ask a woman."

Where we're heading if we don't support each other: Citing a quip from Madeleine Albright, Representative

Carolyn Maloney (D-NY) says, "There is a special place in Hell for women who don't help other women."

The most important secrets to success that I have learned over the course of my career in the entertainment industry are easy for any woman to remember, whether she is still in college or she is a senior executive.

Listen: All perspectives and opinions should be valued and respected, no matter who they come from. A good leader listens to diverse points of view before making a decision.

Be kind: Treat all people, no matter who they are or what their title is, with respect and kindness, just the way you would want to be treated.

Build relationships: In addition to hard work and good performance, women should never underestimate the power of relationships when it comes to career advancement and personal fulfillment at work.

While it has taken the greater part of our careers for many of us to learn some of our most important lessons, we don't want it to take the next generation so long. The Summit was created to unlock these secrets and enable the young Future Frontrunners contest winners to achieve even greater success by building on the momentum created by some of the foremost women leaders in the country.

It was beyond inspiring to see the awe and excitement of these young women when they got to visit the convention floor. There was also a sense of urgency at the Summit to quickly cultivate these young women for leadership. Today, women hold only 17 percent of the seats in Congress, 7 out of 50 governorships, 24.3 percent of state legislatures, and are ranked 71st internationally in women's political representation, behind even Iraq and Afghanistan. Fifteen Fortune 500 companies, or 3 percent, are run by women, and women hold only 3 percent of top positions in mainstream media.

Several of our Future Frontrunners and speakers mentioned the "18 million cracks in the glass ceiling" that Hillary Clinton so famously touted as a symbol of how close a woman had come to holding the highest office in the land (regardless of whether or not they supported her presidential candidacy). But many also lamented that despite this and other examples of progress, there is indeed still a ceiling barring us from changing these statistics.

So when we returned home from the convention, and when the glaring spotlight was removed from the historic candidacies of now secretary of state Hillary Clinton and former governor Sarah Palin, Lifetime and our friends at Voice realized that if we are ever going to crash through that ceiling altogether, it's not enough to let only a handful of women at a time in on the secrets. We wanted to share them far and wide so that women and girls everywhere could benefit and so we could reach a critical mass. Because, as Marie Wilson, the founder and president of The

White House Project, writes, "If we keep running one at a time . . . we will continue to be viewed through the lens of gender, not seen and valued for our agendas." That is why Lifetime is proud to be donating the proceeds from this book to The White House Project to expand their "Go Run" trainings, equipping future women candidates with the skills to run . . . and win.

We are extremely grateful to the contributors to this book who took the time to turn their Future Frontrunners Summit remarks into the essays that follow. They are powerful role models and continue to pave the way for us to have a platform, make changes, and pursue our dreams.

For any men who may pick up this tome, please know that our purpose is not to debate the effectiveness of male versus female leadership. To paraphrase Marie Wilson, to be for women is *not* to be against men. Taking her thoughts one step further, we all have much to gain by enhancing women's leadership. The bottom line is that we need more women in power because, as Representative Shelley Moore Capito (R-WV) affirms, "Good policy depends on input from a wide variety of views and perspectives."

A final note: This is a book of essays by political leaders, born from the political conventions that took place during a historic presidential election season. It is clear from the contributors' stories of policies they have been able to influence and enact that politics is a place where change happens. But you can make change from anywhere, and we hope you use this book as a guide to leadership in any arena you choose.

One of the central themes echoed in the following pages is, don't wait to be asked to lead. *This* is *your* moment. As this book confirms, and as Laurie Westley of the Girl Scouts of the USA writes in her essay, "There's a chorus of women rooting for your success."

secrets of
powerful women

Rosario Dawson, activist and co-founder of Voto Latino,
speaking at the 2008 DNC Women's Caucus in Denver, Colorado

Introduction:
Let's Give Them Something
to Talk About . . . Power

Rosario Dawson

While most people know me as an actress and singer, one of things I'm most proud to be is an activist. As a woman and as a Latina, I am passionate about helping women and Latinos find their voice and use that powerful tool in their political process. That's why, in 2004, I cofounded Voto Latino, an organization dedicated to empowering American Latinos in the United States through registering voters, then encouraging them to vote and get involved in the political process.

Latinos are the fastest-growing demographic in America right now—50,000 Latinos turn eighteen every month, and almost 98 percent of those young adults are eligible to vote (yet only 1 in 6 do). In a democracy, such a large population deserves meaningful representation, yet many American Latinos are still severely shortchanged when it comes to educational opportunities and health care. Voto Latino seeks to bring attention to this solvable problem—and that starts by helping the growing Latino population to participate and engage in their communities and our country. When we go door-to-door and register people to vote, we're telling them, "You are powerful, you have a voice. Don't hold back. Use your voice and make a difference."

But Latinos aren't the only Americans who are not utilizing their growing power. Women make up 51 percent of the population in the United States, and by the time you read these words, women will have surpassed men in number in the American workforce. Yes, women will be the majority of the workforce in this country. Yet conditions like unequal pay are still a stark reality in many working women's lives. In the United States, women are more likely to vote than men, yet we remain underrepresented in our government and in leadership positions across the business world. For example, women and people of color own less than 5 percent of television and radio stations. They make up less than 25 percent of the U.S. House of Representatives.

So many women I've looked up to, from Rita Moreno to Jane Fonda to Eve Ensler, aside from being great dancers, singers, writers, and actors, are also great humanitarians and activists for causes they believe in. I love being an actress, I feel blessed to work with talented actors like Will Smith and Ed Norton, but my work as an activist is what makes me most proud. I believe that my work registering voters is a responsibility. I know it makes my mom and grandmother proud, too. They motivate me to go out there and ask people to respect their power and find their voice. Even on the days I've been rejected ten times in a row, it's all worth it whenever I get even one more person to say yes and register.

Through this process—knocking on doors, approaching people in the street—I've recognized a strength in myself. Each of us has to find her own strengths to understand her power. My power is that I am a recognizable face and voice, and can help draw attention to issues and to people who haven't yet found their voice. I have spoken on many panels and addressed many groups, and I've often been told I should run for office myself. Friends call me Senator Dawson, and that cracks me up. While I have no desire to run for office myself, I find joy in exercising my civic duty by going out and telling people that *they* are powerful. I was raised by strong people who didn't necessarily have great titles but who were powerful in life. Their generosity in encouraging me, in advocating for me, is something I can also do for other people.

What is your strength?

Often, when Voto Latino registers someone in their thirties or forties and it's their first time voting, we ask why they've never voted, and they say it's because no one ever asked them. When Marie Wilson, president of The White House Project, asks why women haven't run for higher office, the answer is the same as when I talk to unregistered Latinos: They are waiting to be asked.

The women sharing their knowledge, stories, and passion in this book are asking you to step up, find your voice—your power—and use it. These women are trailblazers and daredevils, like Madeleine Kunin, the first woman

governor of Vermont, and Loretta Sanchez, the first Latina to serve on the House Judiciary Committee. They
are Congresswomen and lobbyists and journalists. They
are Republicans and Democrats. They are from Tennessee and Washington State, from Texas and Vermont, from
rural Colombia and New York City. They are white, black,
Asian, and Latino. All their stories are stories of passion—
and all the insights into power they share here are culled
from enthusiasm and adventure. These women are relat-
ing their experience of becoming leaders, but their words
are only one half of a conversation. I hope you will want to
talk back to them—to the world—with your actions. Voting is the first, fundamental step. But after we have shown
up at the polls, some of us should consider taking the next
step. And then the next and the next and the next. Into
leadership positions . . . into power.

What is your next step?

Throughout this book, women leaders share their favorite quote, the one that keeps them going. Michelle Bernard
cites one by Marianne Williamson: "Our deepest fear is not
that we are inadequate. Our deepest fear is that we are
powerful beyond measure." If you start acquainting yourself with your own power, you will see that there is little to
no fear. There's such a reservoir of power among us when
we pool our resources and uplift one another. We are limit-
less in our power when we understand that. And that's why
it's so important that we *talk* about power together. It's incredible to hear the stories, the passion that comes out of us.

The endurance of women is like nothing I've ever seen.
I'm blown away by the strength of my grandmother, who

raised five children alone. We need to understand that women are this world's precious resource, and to see to it that every woman and child is safe to walk the streets and take her dreams to the top. We have to get past the point where we diminish one another. During the 2008 presidential race, the campaigns of Hillary Clinton and Sarah Palin were both undermined by the derogatory words journalists wrote about these candidates' wardrobes and demeanor—and many of the journalists who wrote these things were women. When we depict one another that way, we're fighting against one another when we should be fighting together. This is not something we can blame on men. It's our doing.

But we can change. To read this book is to know that change is possible. Almost every woman here was profoundly inspired by a mother (or aunt or grandma) who worked in a time and place when it was unusual for women to work—and they all comment on the importance of these pioneers having opened the door for the rest of us. The same is true for me. I grew up in a squat on the Lower East Side in New York City. My mom got pregnant with me at sixteen. We were poor for my entire childhood, and I wasn't able to go to college because we couldn't afford it. But my mom worked. She cleaned and found work doing freelance carpentry and plumbing. And my mom has always been an activist. These days she's using her carpentry and plumbing skills at her boyfriend's medical clinic in the Dominican Republic. She's also using her activist experience and people skills to help raise money for the clinic. Because of my mom, I've recognized women's resourcefulness and our interconnectedness as a populace since I was very, very young. That's one of the reasons I'm so passionate about being an advocate—I was raised that way. Having that understanding is almost like speaking a different language, and I'm very fluent in it. So I try to encourage other people to learn that language and find their voice.

If your mother amazed you, you will relate to the women who share their stories here—and you'll see the kind of wonderful lives such mothering inspires. If your mother wasn't able to be a role model, if your mother didn't inspire you, then you especially should take up this book. These women are offering their strength and good humor. Take it all. It's yours.

Local Girl Does Good

Kathy Lantry

St. Paul City Council president
and its only woman member

Love Thy Neighborhood

I grew up in the 1960s and had one of the few moms in my neighborhood who worked outside the home. She was a secretary and my dad was a bricklayer. I felt like I had a very normal childhood, though looking back, I don't know if that was the case. My dad was an active union member and it seemed like we were always boycotting some product or manufacturer who was not treating their workforce with dignity. We didn't buy grapes or strawberries because the migrant workers who picked them didn't have bathrooms. It was our way of showing solidarity.

My sister and I were taught from a young age that we had a prominent place in the world. We were taught to have strong opinions about everything. While other families were talking about work and school around the dinner table, we talked about politics. We always knew our state representative, state senator, and county commissioners, not to mention the federal officeholders. We worked for them by dropping literature or organizing door-knock sessions. We traveled by bus to campaign for Hubert Humphrey for president in 1968. We had fund-raisers at our house all the time.

When I was eleven years old, a fast-food chain wanted to rezone a parcel of ground in our neighborhood. My mother organized hundreds of people to fight the rezoning. We made posters and drew up petitions and brought people down to city hall by the busload. Watching all this left a lasting impression on me. In the end, the chain did go in, but as part of a compromise, they purchased a large tract of land on the same street and designated it as open space for the neighborhood. To this day, that open space remains.

"She's My Mom"

Both my mom and dad had worked for St. Paul City Council members, so it seemed natural that when our state senator left to become St. Paul's police chief, my mom ran for his seat. In 1980, there were only six women in the Minnesota Senate out of sixty-seven seats. The area where we lived had never elected a woman, and a lot of people said to her, "That's really cute, but you're never going to make it." But she won. She worked so hard for that seat! Watching her take the time to knock on every door in the district was inspiring. I had recently graduated from high school, and I spent most of that summer door-knocking with her. I loved the chance to talk politics with anyone who would listen. I had T-shirts made that said VOTE FOR MARILYN on the front, and on the back, SHE'S MY MOM.

I first ran for public office in 1995, when my children were nine and six years old. I had never thought about running until I noticed how the incumbent city council member was voting. As I complained about this, the voice in the back of my head came forward loud and clear: If you see something you don't like, *do* something about it.

I worked full-time. My husband worked full-time too. The incumbent had been in office for four years and had long-term connections in the neighborhood. But so did I. Following the example my mom had set, I door-knocked every day as soon as I got home from work. My husband and kids helped by dropping literature and being a wonderful support for me. I lost that first election by 400 votes, but the urge to be in elected office was very strong. In 1998, the seat became open and I ran again. This time I won with over 70 percent of the vote.

We're *All* Agents of Change

The city of St. Paul has a history of electing women to the city council. Unfortunately, I have spent six of my ten years on the seven-person council as the only woman. I did have a reprieve for about four years when another woman got elected, but she was defeated last time, so it's back to me and six male colleagues.

When I go back and look at my contributor list from my first campaign, they're all relatives or friends. When you're starting out, that core of friends and family is where it's at. Certainly I've gotten to know a broader range of people since I was elected. But as I knock on doors now, I still see people I graduated from grade school with or their parents. I've always said that the best thing about representing the neighborhood I grew up in is that I know everybody, and the worst thing is also that I know everybody. I'll be at church, and during the sign of peace someone will say, "Can you get that tree trimmed on my boulevard?" That's life in local politics.

Chances are, presidential candidates are not going to make a personal visit to your house. But if you live in Ward Seven in St. Paul, I've been at your house. I've knocked on your door. The things that have the most direct impact on your life—whether it's your city taxes, or who plows your streets, or whether the cops come when you call—all those things are at my level.

I've been successful in my job because I love what I do. I want to make a difference in how people experience living, working, and playing in the city of St. Paul. I have been in office for ten years and I still look forward to coming to work every day and working toward the elusive goal of making everyone happy.

A Woman's Approach

I think men and women wield power differently. In many cases, there's a greater degree of inflexibility in how men decide things. Once they've made up their minds, that's the end of it. I am always willing to be flexible and to look at multiple ways to accomplish goals. On the council, I'm often the one who says, "Let's sit down and figure out how to get at least half a loaf if we can't accomplish the whole thing." And people will say, "Okay, we'll do that, but we're going to give the credit to somebody else." I don't care. My attitude is, let's just get it done.

First, Be a Volunteer

Before I got elected to the city council, I was on the district council. I coached my sons' soccer and T-ball teams. I was on the church committee. That's how I got to hear what people were talking about—and know what issues were important to them.

Which brings me to my second point: Be a good listener. Taking the time to listen to the hopes, dreams, and fears of those you want to serve will help you prioritize the things that need to be addressed.

Third, have a strong support system. I would not be able to do this job without my husband's backing and encouragement. My kids, who basically grew up during my political life, have always understood how important my job is. And my girlfriends keep me grounded and remind me that I'm just like everyone else—that we are *all* busy and important people.

Beware the Sycophants

When you're in a position to make decisions, a lot of people will tell you how great you are in an effort to promote their own agendas. It's very easy to get caught up in hearing lovely things said about you. Do the right thing because you *believe* it's the right thing, not because someone else praises you. And make sure you surround yourself with people who will be truthful with you.

Don't Take the Stereotypes Personally

It's easier for women to be elected to public office today than when I started out. In Minnesota we have some strong organizations that have made it their mission to elect women. In fact, the very first check I received in my first campaign came from such an organization. Raising money can be difficult, so having that initial boost of financial support is extremely important.

There is still a bias against women in politics. And while at the city council level I may see less of it, I fight the stereotypes all women face. If I'm firm and express what I want, I am the ultimate *B* word. If I make suggestions on how to do things differently, I'm being a mom. I've learned to live with this stereotyping and have decided not to take it personally. But I have also learned not to let it hold me back.

When Protest Leads to Treats

When I was about ten years old, I went to the little convenience store and gas station near my house. I noticed a contest where you could submit your name for a chance to win a new car. I promptly filled out the form. The store manager told me I needed to be at least eighteen years old to enter. I asked him to show me where it said that on the display. It wasn't there, but he told me I still could not enter. When my mom came home from work that day, I told her all about the great injustice that had been perpetrated against me. She told me to write a letter to the corporate headquarters of the gas station and tell them what happened. So I did, and my mom helped me find out where to send my complaint. About a week later, I received a large package in the mail. It contained a letter from the company apologizing for my experience. They explained that they would be sure the display sign listed the age prohibition. But the best part of this package (for a ten-year-old) was all the candy loaded inside it! I still remember my mom telling me that things would change only if I took action, and that this responsibility should not be passed along to someone else.

Small Changes, Meaningful Changes

Over the years I have had the opportunity to influence many city policies and practices, but one memory stands out. An elderly constituent called to complain that a city bus stop had been moved. Although the new stop was only one block farther from her home, she was eighty-nine and felt she wouldn't be able to get there. I contacted the public transit organization, and even though I have no jurisdiction over them, I told them who I was and how important this change was to this older woman. The transit organization agreed to move the bus stop, and when

I called to tell the woman, she told me I had changed her life. All in all, a good day's work.

POWER DRESSING

When my mother got elected to the Minnesota State Senate in 1980, she wasn't allowed to wear pants. When I think back on the times I went door-knocking with her, I remember that she always wore a skirt and looked just lovely. When I went door-knocking, I had on shorts, tennis shoes, and a T-shirt that said KATHY LANTRY FOR CITY COUNCIL. At work these days, I always feel more authoritative in a nice black pantsuit with a plain white blouse. Because women have so many more choices in clothing and accessories, the chances of being judged by those choices increase. Women's choices in clothes should be judged no differently in politics than in real life: If you like it, compliment it, and if you don't, be quiet.

My words for young women

Get your satisfaction from the great things you accomplish, and don't worry about who gets the credit.

That Something in Your Belly

Betsy Myers

Senior Adviser, Barack Obama's presidential campaign ·
Chair, Women for Obama · Chief Operating Officer,
Obama for America · Former Executive Director,
Center for Public Leadership at the Kennedy School
of Government, Harvard University

The Other Side of Fear

What's that something in your belly that gets you out of
bed every morning?

I've never wanted to live an average life. I didn't know
exactly what that meant when I was a young woman, but
I knew I wanted to make a contribution. I wanted my
footprints to matter. My career has spanned politics, aca-
demics, and business—including working in the White
House for President Clinton, running a leadership center
at Harvard University, and being chief operating officer
of the Obama for America presidential campaign.

Looking back on my twenty-five years in the career
world, I think the biggest thing women get in trouble with
is fear. Fear is something we have at every age, and it
keeps us from doing exactly what we want to do.

When I was on the road with the Obama campaign, my family moved to Boston, and my daughter, Madison, went to a new kindergarten. She wanted to take her lunch every day even though they served hot lunches. I was traveling a lot, and one day I forgot to go out and buy bread, so I told Maddy she'd have to have the hot lunch. This sent her into a full-blown meltdown. I knelt so I could look her in the eyes and said, "Are you afraid? Are you afraid to get hot lunch?" She nodded and admitted she didn't know how to do it. She cried all the way to school. And then her wonderful teacher took her by the hand, explained how it worked, and assigned her a hot lunch buddy. That night I asked Madison about hot lunch. She said, "Mommy, I learned how to do it and I want to do it again tomorrow." Now she gets hot lunch most every day.

There are two things I want to teach my daughter. One is to be a kind person. At the end of the day, that matters more than how successful you are. The other thing is that when you're afraid, it's a sign that you need to push through the fear. Whether we are six or sixty, we all have fears of the unknown. I always ask myself, "What's the worst thing that can happen?" I could fail—and that's not life or death. Or maybe I'll find out that this new endeavor is something I don't like. These are things you learn from. The biggest growth experiences in my life have happened when I pushed through my fear.

The universe presents new jobs, new relationships, and new opportunities that may shake up your life. And just as Madison learned, we gain personal confidence when we push beyond our comfort zone. I would never have reached the levels of my career without taking risks and seizing new opportunities. Each job adventure pushed me and shaped me into the person I am today, bringing a deeper understanding of what makes me happy and most productive. I have come to appreciate that life is really a process of self-discovery and we never have it figured out. That's the big secret. We never stop having decisions to make, hurdles to jump. This is what it means to be human; it's the process of learning to be our authentic selves.

When I joined the Obama for America Campaign as chief operating officer in January 2007, it was an opportunity to play a key role in a historic campaign. I've always loved start-up challenges and putting teams together. But the day-to-day work of being a COO—budgets, office space, personnel, and legal issues—did not make my heart sing. I've always flourished in jobs where I interact with people in a liaison and outreach function. One of my favorite jobs was serving as the director of the White House Office for Women's Outreach for President Clinton. I already knew this about myself, but now I understand it more deeply. So, even though it wasn't the job that fit me most perfectly, I would never trade my campaign COO experience and the clarity that it brought me.

Words I live by

"Do the thing you fear most."
—ELEANOR ROOSEVELT

Your Personal Advisory Board

I'm a big believer in having mentors. We can't know everything, and it never serves us well to act as if we do. It's important to have truth tellers in your life who will keep you honest—girlfriends often play this role. Mentors can come from both our personal and professional lives. They don't have all the answers, but they do have insights.

Over time, you develop a personal advisory board. And sometimes it's good to consult people who are not so close to you because the closer people are to you, the more they're emotionally invested in you. A coach who's a little more distant can be more truthful. I have a coach—someone I met through my work at Harvard—who is a strategic thinker. I talk to her every few months to get her take on recent events in my life.

The best leaders are lifelong learners; they seek out people to listen to and learn from. Each of us faces the challenge of identifying our individual contribution to the world. As one dear friend of mine asks, "What is the pearl we are adding to the universe?" We all know that feeling when we are doing something in our life that doesn't seem right for us. We must create space in our lives to listen to ourselves about what makes us happy and fulfilled along the journey of our one precious life.

How Do Women Lead? Differently.

Women bring a different dynamic to leadership, one that's more instinctively team-centered. We also bring a female perspective to policy making. It is very important that women's voices are heard and represented in government and our political system. We've come a long way, but we have a long way to go.

I was attracted to politics because I believed it was an important way to make a difference in the world. Public service leadership positions enabled me to have input and authority around policy, programs, and budgets that had a positive impact for women and small-business owners. These positions often give you a much larger reach of people you can help compared to other public service opportunities. It's incredibly meaningful work and brings the opportunity to do much good in the world. Having political experience also gives you insights about what has and hasn't worked in the past.

How to Stand Out in a Crowded Talent Pool

Most young people enter politics at the assistant level, and that's where you build your relationship foundation and professional reputation. How you return calls, treat people, and deal with difficult situations is critical to representing your boss and your organization. The four key lessons for young people are very simple: Become an expert in your job or policy area. Become known as someone who has a positive attitude and is wonderful to work with. Become very diligent on follow-up and follow-through. And begin to build your lifelong relationship network and team of mentors.

When I was in the White House I got to pick ten interns. One young woman, who I'll never forget, noticed that I had a dead plant in my office, or almost dead. So she got a cup and watered it. I thought, *This is a kid to watch.* She was always thinking about ways she could make my life better. She impressed me so much that I took her to meetings in the White House that other interns didn't get to attend. There are a lot of smart, capable young people who are given the opportunity to work for powerful people. What will set you apart is to make yourself indispensable, even if it means doing grunt work.

Be Tough—It's Not Personal

Don't be oversensitive. One of the biggest lessons I have learned in my career is that 99 percent of life is not personal. When we're not invited to a meeting or someone is less than kind, we often attribute it to something about us. We create a story in our head, and often share it with co-workers, thus wasting time and energy on something that is not productive. Often what really happened is that someone had a bad day, or had something on their mind, or it was simply an oversight. Staying above the fray with razor-sharp focus on your job is the key to success. This is not to say you should never address a misunderstanding, or that you won't find difficult people in the workplace. But be careful about what drama you may be creating in your own head and in your workplace.

The New Normal

My first campaign was the Mondale-Ferraro presidential campaign in 1984. I was so excited that we had the first woman, Geraldine Ferraro, as the vice presidential candidate. Twenty-four years later, Hillary Clinton was a serious contender to be the first woman president of the United States. My six-year-old daughter's first memory of a presidential election will be one with a woman and an African-American. She will grow up with a totally different perception of what is normal and realistic for women to achieve.

I remember so clearly when President Clinton appointed Madeleine Albright as the first woman secretary of state. The White House was flooded with phone calls and letters of excitement from around the world. I asked the president if he was surprised by the outpouring. He remarked that he was indeed, as he had chosen Madeleine not because she was a woman but because she was the most qualified. Now a woman as secretary of state seems quite normal. The world has watched as Condoleezza Rice and Hillary Clinton follow in Madeleine Albright's footsteps. We have already seen President Obama appoint many women and people of color to his administration. He made a strong statement by choosing equal pay for women as his first bill. What other glass ceilings will he shatter for women?

When My Mother Found Her Voice

My mother went back to school to finish her undergraduate degree and get her master's in psychology when I was a teenager. I observed how this changed her life and the dynamics of our family; my father had to take more responsibility for me and my sisters at night.

My mother went on to run women's reentry programs at the local junior college. Her decision to gain her voice in the world had a profound impact on me. Her journey and the stories she shared with me about her students awakened me to the realities of our world and the struggles many women face. She inspired my passion for women's issues and women's leadership, which has been a factor in every stage of my career. My mother also taught me that we have the personal power to change the roles we play in our lives by a lifelong commitment to personal growth.

Small Loans, Big Lessons

As the director of women's business ownership at the U.S. Small Business Administration, I helped create a new lending program for women business owners called the prequalification loan program. It helped thousands of women get loans who had previously been rejected. By supporting these women entrepreneurs with the right management and technical assistance, we were able to guide them through the process from their loan application to eventual approval. As I traveled the country, I met many of the women whose lives had been changed for the better because of their ability to get a business loan. Their success as business owners—and the positive impact on their employees, families, and communities—was my first real tangible experience with the difference one can make in government.

POWER DRESSING

Just as a twelve-second scan of your resume makes an impression, so does a twelve-second scan of your appearance in a job interview. I have watched smart, beautiful women be marginalized due to their choice of inappropriate clothes in the workplace. Be aware of how you present yourself in the world. Do you appear put together and organized, or disheveled and frazzled? It does matter. It makes a statement about who you are. I personally feel powerful in the classy/eloquent look that works well as we age. As women, we are often too busy to take care of ourselves, leaving exercise, manicures, and routine brow waxing behind. I challenge us to make time in our schedules for upkeep that makes us feel more put together and confident.

My words for young women

Bloom where you are planted. If you concentrate on being excellent in the job you have, someone will notice. You often see people plotting their next job opportunity before they have established themselves in the current situation. Senior members of an organization are always looking for talent and notice those in the ranks who are honest, loyal, dedicated to excellence, and willing to go above and beyond expectations. Ask yourself: How can I best support my boss today and make his/her life easier? What can I do today to support the organization's goal? This awareness will enable you to focus on the most important aspects of your job and contribute in ways that will create your next opportunity.

Our Struggle Is Not Over

Martha Burk

Co-founder, Center for Advancement of Public Policy ·
Director, Corporate Accountability Project for the National
Council of Women's Organizations (NCWO) ·
Money editor, *Ms. Magazine*; syndicated newspaper columnist;
author, *Your Money and Your Life* and *Cult of Power* ·
Senior Policy Adviser for Women's Issues to Governor
Bill Richardson of New Mexico

Beyond the "Golden Age"

I grew up in a time that's often idealized as a "golden age" of the twentieth century, the late 1940s and 1950s. World War II was over, there was a lot of pent-up demand for goods, and jobs were plentiful. Families could live on one salary, and women were sent home from their wartime jobs to tend home and hearth. We now know, of course, that this age was not so golden for women. Many felt trapped and isolated, and a great deal of talent went to waste as women stayed out of the workforce due to societal pressure.

My mother and grandmother ignored the social dictates of the time and worked outside the home. In my suburban, white, middle-class school, there was some stigma attached to having a mother who worked. But now I realize these women were strong lifelong role models for me.

This was also a time when families who could afford to send their kids to college thought that only their sons should be educated. After all, they were going to be breadwinners, while the girls were destined for marriage and family. Thank goodness my family did not subscribe to this dictate either. Though I married as an eighteen-year-old college sophomore in 1960, I graduated with a B.S. in psychology in 1962.

I went on to earn both a master's degree and a doctorate while the mother of two young children. It was a very challenging and sometimes difficult time in my life. While I loved my children and was devoted to them, I didn't feel I was reaching my potential. My husband was a workaholic and not available to help with the kids, though he did provide financial support. I took a job as a teaching assistant to afford in-home care for the kids and give me some measure of independence.

My work with the National Council of Women's Organizations (NCWO) did not begin until I had raised my two sons and started a successful computer software business. I had always worked on women's issues as a hobby, and it became a passion I wanted to devote all my time to. By then I was married to my second husband, also a social activist. We moved to Washington, D.C., and started a nonprofit organization dedicated to corporate accountability and advancement for women. As head of a member organization in the NCWO, I became integrated into this national sisterhood of groups working on a whole spectrum of women's issues, from abortion rights to child care to social security to violence against women.

In time, I was elected chair of the NCWO. Though the membership consisted of over one hundred women's groups, the staff was small and the budget meager for a national organization. I did not get paid, even though it was more than a full-time job. We worked on many campaigns, including helping to stop the privatization of Social Security, increasing child care for poor women, preserving affirmative action, and getting the universal women's human rights treaty ratified. The heads of our organizations collaborated closely with the White House Office on Women's Issues during the Clinton years, but President Bush abolished the office when he took charge.

Words I live by

Emma Goldman, the early-twentieth-century labor activist, said, "If I can't dance, I won't come to your revolution." I like to think she wasn't talking only about inclusion but also about the need to keep a positive outlook in working for social change and not just concentrate on the negative.

It Was About Sexism—Not Golf

In 2003 I had been chair of the NCWO for three years, and I was thinking about not running for reelection, since

I believe the effectiveness of a leader in any organization diminishes with time. But then the national controversy over allowing women into the Augusta National Golf Club exploded in the media, and I was at the center of it. The club tried to run me out of office, hiring a public relations firm to discredit me, and calling the member groups to try and get me ousted. I couldn't let them banish me as the organization leader, and the groups stood solidly behind me. By the time the controversy was finally out of the public eye, two more years had passed. I knew it was time to make a change, so I told the NCWO steering committee I wanted to leave as chair but stay involved.

I am now the director of the Corporate Accountability Task Force for the NCWO. We formed a partnership with a national civil rights law firm right after the Augusta controversy, to investigate sex discrimination in the firms whose CEOs are members of the golf club. We heard from women who worked for these companies, and they told us that the problems went much deeper than just one golf club membership. Sex discrimination in the workplace is one area where the trickle-down theory works: If top management tolerates it, then frontline managers think it's okay too. To date we have facilitated two class-action lawsuits, and the women in these companies have collected a total of $79 million in settlements against charges of sex discrimination. I am very proud of this project. Even though we did not succeed in opening the golf club to women, we are helping women advance in other ways and teaching them that they do not have to tolerate unequal treatment at work.

The advice I would give the next generation is this: Don't ever think the struggle is over. If there is anything I have learned in my life's journey so far it is that there will always be people who think women are and should be second-class citizens. Feminists in the twentieth century made great strides. But as long as there are forces working against fundamental equality and trying to roll back our progress, we have to be on guard to make sure our daughters and granddaughters don't lose those hard-won gains. The bottom line: Stay involved, stay informed, and always work for the betterment of women.

See the Big Picture

At first, I worked to change outcomes for individual women, and that's important. I later came to realize, though, that fundamental change in society and law could make a systemic difference for all women, so I started to work on the big picture. I do think powerful women are still viewed differently from men: If we're too assertive, we're characterized as "bitchy" and "castrating"—we all saw how the press treated Hillary Clinton during her presidential run. This doesn't mean we can't be assertive and push hard. We just have to smile more while we're doing it.

Failure Is Fine, but Line Up Some Powerful Friends

You don't need as much experience as you think you do. It's often said that women don't run for office because they don't think they have the experience, and men just get elected and figure out how to do the job later. I think young women should be as well informed as possible, but don't hold back because you've never held office. If you run and lose, the experience can be valuable the next time around. And don't think you have to hold five or six low-level offices over twenty years before going for something higher. This is one area where we can learn from men.

Another piece of advice: It's a sad fact that money talks in getting elected. Line up "angels" who can help you get where you want to go. There are many women with money who will help—but they have to be asked.

It's very tempting to compromise your principles to please a donor. I've always let donors know exactly who I am and what I and my organizations stand for before I take money from them. That way they won't be asking you to modify your positions later, or to keep your mouth shut when you should be speaking up. Being honest with yourself is most important. If you can't preserve that, you can't be effective as a change agent.

We're Not Going Anywhere

When I came out of college in 1962, the only women in politics were taking the places of their dead husbands. Now it is normal for women to seek the highest offices, and I don't think any president would consider an all-male cabinet, which was the norm for so much of our history. Gone are the days when women could only be typists and closet advisers behind the scenes, when the occasional woman in high office was seen as some kind of sideshow. We have already smashed the barriers in every lower level of government, though we are far from 50 percent representation. Women in politics are here to stay, thank goodness.

I Come from a Line of Iconoclasts

All the women in my childhood—my mother, my grandmother, and my aunts—were powerful role models. Though they were born at a time when working outside the home was frowned on if the family could afford to live on one salary, they all ignored that and worked anyway. They started a successful business and everybody pitched in. In our family there was always a quest for excellence, and my mother pushed all of us kids to do our best and use our minds to reach higher. My grandmother taught me the importance of unconditional love, and that even if you are not formally educated you can make a positive contribution to society. I can't leave my dad out here. He was also a very strong role model, teaching me compassion and the value of meaningful work.

Entrenched Power Imbalances

I was leading the oldest and largest coalition of women's groups in the United States, and we were very influential in Washington politics. We learned that the Augusta National Golf Club, whose members were a powerful cadre of men from America's largest corporations, did not allow women. We thought that was wrong because it sent a message that no matter how well women did in business, they were not the equals of men, and our most powerful CEOs were condoning it.

After a yearlong battle that played out in the national press, we were unsuccessful in getting the club to change. The "boys" all stuck together. Not one CEO had the courage to say the policy was wrong, or resign in protest. That taught me that political power may not be enough when you are fighting ingrained social attitudes. Some men were so worked up about it that I had threats on my life for challenging the power structure. The whole experience reminded me that we still have a long way to go. But in a sense that lesson was the victory: Women around the country realized that we're not as equal as we think we are, and I know it energized many to keep working for change.

POWER DRESSING

I have never subscribed to the idea that women should be able to wear anything they want and still be taken seriously. I think men learned this lesson long ago: If *they* showed up for work with their midriffs hanging out, we wouldn't take them seriously either. To me, there is nothing more powerful than a well-cut black suit, either with pants or a skirt. It can go anywhere. I know there's an ongoing debate among feminists about high heels and how they're a throwback to another era.

Well, they are. If I had saved all those shoes I wore in the fifties, I wouldn't ever have to shop for shoes again. There's nothing wrong with high heels if they make you feel powerful. Just be sure they match the occasion and are appropriate for the rest of the outfit—red open-toed sling-backs have a way of killing that power look.

My words for young women

Don't say or do anything you wouldn't want to see on YouTube. We're never out of the public spotlight in this electronic age.

The Girl Who Loved Politics

Laurie Westley

Senior vice president, Public Policy, Advocacy, and the
Research Institute, Girl Scouts of the USA · Former chief
counsel and staff director, U.S. Senate Judiciary
Committee · Former assistant counsel, U.S. House of
Representatives Postsecondary Education Subcommittee

My Inside Job

My path was one of passion, absolute passion. I found it in
high school. I was the black sheep in my family—the one
who loved politics.

As a schoolgirl in the early 1960s, I learned that only
one woman was serving in the U.S. Senate: Margaret Chase
Smith of Maine. My teacher spoke reverently of her achieve-
ments, noting that she was the first woman ever to be elected
to both the House and the Senate. Margaret Chase Smith
seemed far removed from my everyday reality. She was on
a pedestal with other women icons—Harriet Tubman,
Amelia Earhart, Eleanor Roosevelt. We were supposed to
admire them, but we were not expected to emulate them.
Girls were tracked to be nurses and teachers, while boys
could run corporations and the government. Yet Smith's

gentle tilt at the status quo made an impression on me: "When people tell you that you can't do a thing, you kind of like to keep trying."

My family acknowledged the importance of civic awareness. Everybody voted, and they believed government was a force for good in people's lives. For example, because of Medicare, my grandfather was able to have open-heart surgery to prolong his life. But though my family wanted me to become civically engaged, they felt that politics was a dirty business best left to others.

I saw it differently. Policies that could improve people's lives were decided by political campaigns. So it was logical to me that combining politics and policy was the best way to serve the public good. Still, during the 1960s, the idea of a woman actually *running* for elected office was not part of the civics lesson. Nor was it part of my initial understanding of a woman's role in the political process. In high school, I was elected to student government positions that allowed me to help set priorities and make decisions. That led me to work on my first political campaign. Although all I was doing was stuffing envelopes, I fell in love.

When I was in college, I moved to Washington, D.C., to co-manage a woman's campaign for city council. They hadn't had a city council in fifty years, so they were willing to take any college kid who'd ever worked on an election. I fell in love with that town that loved politics and policy as much as I did.

When I graduated from law school, there was no way I was going to a law firm. I wanted to use my degree to influence policy and make the world a better place. I knew I could do more if I worked to change the laws, not just debate their interpretation in the courts. So I followed a very traditional Washington path: I worked on Capitol Hill. I ran a Senate judiciary subcommittee and then spent years working in women's organizations, Senate campaigns, and presidential campaigns.

Words I live by

Lift up your eyes upon
The day breaking for you.
Give birth again
To the dream.

—MAYA ANGELOU,
from "On the Pulse of Morning"

Make Sure You Feel Good When You Wake Up in the Morning

I wish I could tell you I never doubted my decision to go into politics, even when my friends were making much more money. But when I did have doubts, I always reminded myself: "Do what you love, and when you get up in the morning, you'll know why."

And I do know why. I've worked in both the House and the Senate. My contributions have changed national policies and helped ensure that government continued to be a force for good. Believing that electing more women would lead to better policies for women and children, I became the political and legislative director for the National Women's Political Caucus. One day, a woman who wanted to run for Texas state treasurer came to meet with me. She was a force—she was smart, said what she meant, had great personal style, and was surrounded by women just like her. Ann Richards changed my sense of what it would take for women to succeed in politics. She was one of my early role models, and as she rose to become governor, she went on to inspire an entire generation of women.

I Am Rooting for Your Success

Today, young women still stuff envelopes for campaigns, but the candidates they support are increasingly likely to be women. Women in government are no longer unreachable icons but true role models.

As a senior vice president at Girl Scouts of the USA and someone who works with members of Congress every day, I witness these members offering optimism and opportunity for girls and women everywhere. They understand that women are urgently needed to bring their unique perspective to the public debate. As the author Carol Gilligan states, "In the different voice of women lies the truth of an ethic of care, the tie between relationship and responsibility." I am proud to see women's voices increasingly shaping the policies that shape our country.

I was raised at a time when women were not encouraged to aim high. Yet so many of us have succeeded. All of us have encountered resistance to our dreams and ideas—not because we lacked intellectual ability, ambition, or charisma, but because we are women. Perhaps our successes have been sweeter because they often came at a high cost. We have been forced to make choices not often required of our male counterparts. Our common experiences create a bond among those of us who manage to achieve a fulfilling blend of home, family, personal growth, and career. My network of women has helped me succeed when I couldn't have done so alone.

I am buoyed by the belief that my generation has cleared obstacles for the next, enabling them to follow their passions and reach for their dreams. I hope they know I'm part of a chorus of women rooting for their success.

Become Your Potential

Be audacious. Dream big. Rejoice in all that you are and want to become. Then step into your potential. Work hard. Take advantage of all your opportunities. Step up to the edge—it's where change happens. You can be anything you want to be!

The World Needs All of Us

I went to law school because I wanted to make the world better, especially for women and girls. I used to feel sheepish saying that; it sounded too bold. Now I derive enormous pleasure in working for the Girl Scouts of the USA, an organization whose mission is to "build girls of courage, confidence and character who make the world a better place."

Political power is often associated with a "command and control" leadership style. But many women have become successful leaders because they embraced a *collaborative* style, which has given them enormous opportunities to make significant changes. We need to embrace our own leadership style. The world needs us.

My Secret Weapons

Four tips that make the bad days okay and the good days even better:

1. Find work you love, work for people you respect and admire, and learn everything you can.
2. Find something outside of work that you love, and don't stop doing it.
3. Be wherever you are 100 percent. When you're at work, be there totally. When you're off, enjoy your time off.
4. Love the fact that your life is full.

Don't Worry If Your Path Is Not Straight

Young women often think there is a clear path, a sequence of career moves that will ensure success. I've found this is not the case. There is no right answer, no single path to your goal. So don't feel you have to plan every aspect of your life. Be open to new opportunities and don't place limits on your dreams. Expect that things may not go

exactly as you've planned. If you're clear about the work
you want to do, stay focused and follow your passion. You
will succeed.

Consider the Question Settled

When I moved to Washington in 1974, there were sixteen
women in the House and zero women in the Senate. In the
111th Congress, which opened in 2009, there were seventy-
seven women in the House and seventeen in the Senate.
Women are taking their place in the centers of power, albeit
rather slowly. Within the last few years, a woman became
Speaker of the House of Representatives. A woman was a
serious contender for her party's presidential nomination.
A woman was her party's vice presidential nominee. The
question is no longer whether women are ready to lead.

The First Time I Was Part of
an Important Change

At thirty-three, I became chief counsel to Senator Paul
Simon on the Senate Judiciary Committee and staff director of a subcommittee. My values and thinking were
aligned with his, so it was easy for me to represent him
on a broad range of Senate legislation and judicial nominations. Senator Simon was asked to lead the Democrats' review process for all judicial nominations. He
took his new role very seriously, and I knew I was going
to be part of a momentous change. His work resulted in
a clearer set of standards and a higher level of scrutiny

of judicial nominations. I loved being a part of this moment in history.

MY DEFINITION OF POWER DRESSING

I love fashionable, classy clothes, and I love to feel totally put together. It gives me an extra burst of confidence. I confess I enjoy observing how other women put their outfits together; it's a great way to get new ideas. But my most important advice is to enjoy your own beauty and don't compare yourself with others.

My words for young women

My mother was a wise and remarkable woman. She taught me many of the life lessons that still serve me well. I'll share three:

1. Like a good Girl Scout, be prepared. Know your goal, and be open to various opportunities and paths to reach it.
2. Take joy in celebrating the success of others. This is sometimes harder than it sounds— and that's when it's a great opportunity to be your best.
3. Maximize your opportunities: Work hard and be true to your values. Never worry about leaving the path everyone else seems to be on.

Stay in the Race

Carolyn Maloney

First woman to represent the 7th City Council District of New York City · First woman to represent the 14th Congressional District of New York · First woman to chair the Joint Economic Committee in Congress · Author, *Rumors of Our Progress Have Been Greatly Exaggerated*

People Laughed at Me—Until I Won

The 2008 presidential campaign was both the best of times and the worst of times for women. Hillary Clinton's campaign lifted up every woman in America and around the world. We are all standing a little taller and prouder because she gained eighteen million votes and raised almost as much money as Barack Obama—the second largest amount in history. She conducted an excellent campaign and won many debates. This was groundbreaking. It was historic. I did a poll on what women voters thought were the most important actions in recent years, and the majority said it was Hillary Clinton's race for president.

On the other hand, it showed a dark side of American politics: misogyny, stereotyping—all the barriers for women

that make the process really unfair. It was outrageous—
and so was the silence among leaders and pundits who
failed to speak out against blatant sexism. Hillary had a
unique set of hurdles that made her quest very, very hard.

Carol Jenkins of the Women's Media Center was outraged at the stereotyping and sexism, but when she called
up her colleagues in the media, they denied it was there.
So she compiled a movie of all these sexist statements and
showed it to them: People called Hillary a castrator in the
eunuch chorus. They said, "Iron my shirt." "Make me a
sandwich." "Get out of the race." One man said that when
he heard her voice, it reminded him of his wife saying,
"Take out the garbage."

This, I remind you, is a distinguished, powerful
woman. A remarkable senator. A former first lady. And
yet they demeaned her constantly. It hinted at the hurdles we have before us. Looking at the contrast between the way men and women are treated, I thought
someone should write a book about this. So I did [*Rumors of Our Progress Have Been Greatly Exaggerated:
Why Women's Lives Aren't Getting Any Easier—and
How We Can Make Real Progress for Ourselves and Our
Daughters*].

Words I live by

One of my favorite quotes in my book is from Madeleine Albright, who said, "There is a special place

in Hell for women who don't help other women." I think that each of us should find some way, large or small, to help another woman.

You Have to Be Your Biggest Advocate

I was born at a time when opportunities were just not there for women. I never dreamed I would be in the United States Congress. But I went out and got to work in politics. First, I was a lobbyist for the board of education. I was lobbying for funding, and I could see that the legislature had more input and influence on the education standards of New York City than the schools chancellor did. So I ran for city council, where I worked for ten years. But during the Reagan/Bush years, aid to New York City was cut by unprecedented numbers—74 percent! And they were rolling back *Roe v. Wade*, clearly intending to overturn it. I said, "This is intolerable. I am going to run for Congress."

Never let someone tell you that you can't do something. What if I had listened to all the people who told me I couldn't run for office? People said, "How dare you run for city council against an incumbent? You'll never win." They tried to throw me out of the race; I spent half my time in court keeping my name on the ballot. When I challenged Bill Green for his seat in Congress, he was a fourteen-year Republican incumbent who outspent me five to one. People laughed at me. But I beat him.

Women Are a Worthy Cause

American women have asked for two fundamental things: the right to vote and equality under the law. I would say, why is everyone surprised that Hillary Clinton didn't win when we can't even get the Equal Rights Amendment written into the Constitution of the United States? It says: "Equality of rights under the law shall not be denied or abridged by the United States or by any state on account of sex." How threatening is that?

I don't think you would find any American who would say that women should be discriminated against. But when you study the numbers, you see that we still earn seventy-seven cents to every dollar men earn. Women are 51 percent of the population, 17 percent of Congress, and only 5 percent of CEOs. Just 3 percent of the clout jobs in media go to women. So there is still a lot of work to be done, and I would challenge you to find a cause or a goal that is as worthy.

Be a mentor. Find a mentor. Get out there and make a difference. Eleanor Roosevelt used to say, "It's up to the women." I truly do believe that with more women at not just the kitchen table, but the peace table, the legislative table, the media table, all the tables of the world—this world will be a better place. It's up to you. Go out there, take your seat at the table, and make a difference with your life.

Wield Power Like a Woman

Power is the opportunity to make real and manifest what you believe deep in your heart. It is the opportunity to affect and improve people's lives, particularly women and children. Unfortunately, it can also be used for ill—to make sure that things are done your way. That can be the ultimate expression of the petty and small-minded pursuit of power. We have all seen too much of that in recent years.

Women tend to wield political power differently from men, in large part because their life experiences are different from those of men. The obstacles and injustices they encounter are often starkly different, and that shapes their awareness and understanding. Take the issue of gender-based pay discrimination, such as the problems addressed in the Lilly Ledbetter Pay Equality Act. A woman who has experienced economic injustice, and understands deeply and keenly how it affects her and her family, may very well give a higher priority to addressing that issue than, say, making golf club dues tax deductible.

Broaden Your Passions

Be passionate about what you believe in—but beware of being tagged as a "one issue" politician. Apply your passion for justice and equality wherever it might be needed. That is one reason I got involved in the Credit Card Holders Bill of Rights legislation. It targets deceptive and

unfair credit card practices, which hurt not just women
and families but single men and businesses as well. It is
important to help people understand that economic injustice hurts us all and can make our country less competitive in a global economy.

"Woman President" Was a Punch Line

I can remember picking up an issue of *Life* magazine
when I was a young girl and reading an interview with
Margaret Chase Smith, the only woman in the United
States Senate at the time. They asked her, "Senator Smith,
what would you do if you woke up in the White House?"
Her response was, "I would apologize immediately to Bess
Truman and leave." If you asked Hillary Clinton that
question today, she would have a whole list of challenges
that we need to address as a nation. So, we have come a
long way. But we still need to go a lot further.

POWER DRESSING

The scrutiny of women—their clothing, their hair,
their laugh, you name it—soared to such ludicrous
heights during Hillary Clinton's presidential
campaign that the stupidity began to get the
mainstream media's attention. It was very
interesting to watch many of my more conservative
male colleagues become suddenly sensitive to this
issue when the same nonsense was directed at
Sarah Palin. People realized how hurtful it could

be, and we may have actually taken a small step forward. But it emphasizes again how important it is to have women in equal numbers on high-profile tickets: This is how society-wide change in perception can be brought about.

All that being said, I do have a great royal blue TV-friendly suit that really takes a string of pearls rather well.

My words for young women

Ask for what you want. Don't wait to be asked, because you won't be. Ask for that raise. Ask for that job. Ask for that promotion. Ask for what want to do in life. If you sit back and wait, it will never come to you. In the many years Democrats were in the minority, I could have written a book on the Zen of losing. I lost more fights on the floor than I can count. But I learned something from each one, and it made me stronger for the next. The only poor choice is not trying in the first place.

If you ever think you can't do something, look at the fools who do.

Speak Out

Susan Bevan

Co-chair, Republican Majority for Choice

It's About the Individual

I've been a Republican since I was in my early teens. Thanks to my parents' involvement in local politics in Washington State, I formed my ideas early. I have always been interested in politics and history, and I believe very strongly in the original Republican ideals of keeping government as small as possible. Republicans traditionally believe in protecting individual freedom, individual rights, and individual opportunity. I believe that individuals know best how to spend their money and take care of their own health. I believe that it is not the place of the government to determine what happens to your body.

It is not Republican to dictate these decisions. It is *certainly* not conservative. Over the past thirty years, the definitions of these words have been eviscerated to the point where Americans now think that if you are Republican and a conservative, you believe the opposite—that the government can and should be involved in the most intimate of decisions. This is because a very vocal minority in the Republican Party (polling consistently shows it to be less than 30 percent of party members) have decided to control these decisions. That minority has worked very hard to change laws throughout the country. I work with the Republican Majority for Choice because we *must* get back to protecting individual autonomy. Our job is to communicate, clearly and strongly, the value of keeping reproductive choices personal.

Words I live by

"Collect experiences, not things."

—GREY WOLF

Protecting Women's Rights Around the World—and at Home

A woman's right to control her reproductive health is absolutely central to our success as a civilization. It's no coincidence that the most successful economic programs throughout the world focus on women's education and entrepreneurship. It's incredibly frustrating to see how members of government, and my own party, work against these tenets by limiting women's options. The world's most repressive regimes target those who would liberate women from the shackles of ignorance or bondage. This includes reproductive "bondage"—and, shockingly, parallels can be drawn in our own country.

Repeated efforts by the Bush Administration compromised the freedom and human dignity of women by restricting their reproductive decisions. U.S. hospitals are able to refuse to give emergency contraception, also known as Plan B, to rape victims in emergency rooms. With the blessing and support of the government, there are anti-choice "counselors" who falsely claim that abortions cause breast cancer, and medical professionals who *refuse* to dispense contraceptives, even with a valid prescription, *even* to married women. Those who would deny women the right to make their own childbearing decisions keep women in virtual reproductive burkas. We need to throw off these metaphorical burkas and continue to speak out.

During the 2008 elections, I saw firsthand how we at the RMC were able to influence ballot measures across the United States. We defeated a "personhood" initiative in Colorado that would have given equal human rights to fertilized eggs, privileging those rights over the mother's. What would have been the outcry if there had been an attempt to give sperm the same rights as men?

A Political Double Standard

Over forty years ago, two very important legal cases, *Griswold v. Connecticut* and *Roe v. Wade*, gave women the freedom to make their own reproductive decisions.

Griswold gave women the right to select their own methods of birth control, and Roe was a watershed decision that gave women full control over their own bodies. It's important to remember that by giving women the opportunity to plan their families, Roe enabled them to participate fully in the social, economic, and political life of our nation.

Try to imagine if government officials dictated to men that they would be forced to have vasectomies—or, conversely, that they were forbidden to have them. Or imagine if men were required to show proof of marriage to a woman of childbearing age before they were allowed to purchase Viagra. Wouldn't men be outraged about the government's interference with their reproductive decisions? It would be ridiculous. But it's painfully real for women.

However, thanks to organizations like the Republican Majority for Choice, Planned Parenthood, and others, there are clinics, nurses, doctors, staff, and volunteers throughout the world who provide services to those who most need them. There are other political organizations that lobby tirelessly for our rights. There are men and women everywhere who are fighting for these same freedoms: the right to make our own decisions for our bodies.

Speak Up to Preserve Our Freedom

To protect these freedoms, it's imperative that each citizen use his or her political voice and vote to ensure the independence of women's reproductive health. One of the most important things we can do is to make our voices heard. It can take as few as five letters from constituents for a legislator to listen to those persuasive voices. By reacting to alarming proposed legislation, constituents could really see some changes in government. Those who have dominated the anti-choices agenda have known this and made their case forcefully for many decades.

The majority of Americans do *not* believe it's the government's place to make reproductive health decisions for others. It's hard to accept that Republican leadership, consisting of those who are otherwise committed to equality and civil rights, is still challenging the basic rights of women. Nobody is in favor of abortions. But victims of rape or incest should not be forced to have children they don't want. This not about being pro-life. *I* am pro-life. I chose to have children. What I am *not* is anti-choice. I don't have to force you to *have* an abortion or *not* have one. All I have to do is let you make that decision for yourself.

Our challenge in the Republican Party is to educate people and find common ground. The Republican Majority for Choice works with federal and state government representatives to craft and pass legislation to protect women's rights to choices. The RMC supports candidates running for office who respect and protect individual freedoms. With the cooperation of other moderate Republican organizations, we hope to bring the Republican Party back to a position of strength. This is more about ideas and freedom, however, than about any one party or brand. Good ideas open doors and freedoms for others, which in turn lift our society as a whole. It's good business—and it's good sense.

Getting Elected Is the First Step

Political power is achieved through consensus building and negotiating, regardless of who seeks to make changes. Political power is simply a means to an end. It serves to influence public policy by engaging friends and colleagues in visions, ideas, and knowledge.

POWER DRESSING

The media demonstrated its uneasiness in covering a shift in power between women and men. The focus on Hillary Clinton's voice and Sarah Palin's eyewear—but not the chin tucks, eyelid lifts, or mole removals of the men—was a particularly low point during the 2008 election. The focus of our media should be about the candidates' positions on issues that affect Americans.

My words for young women

Never compromise on your values. You must be willing to stand up for your beliefs, willing to lose a race or an election, in order to have credibility. Be prepared to learn from others, and always look for new ways to enhance your understanding of the issues. A debate with an opponent may strengthen your beliefs—or change them for the better.

Head with Heart

Susan Wolf Turnbull

Former vice chair, Democratic National Committee (DNC) ·
Chair, Maryland Democratic Party ·
Chair, Board of Trustees of Jewish Women International ·
Community activist for more than 25 years

Politics Matters

The Democratic National Committee, made up of 447 men and women from all fifty states, is in charge of the nominating process for the party—the resolutions and platform—and making sure the party's message gets out. As vice chair, I'm a full-time volunteer—more than full-time.

I grew up in Cleveland Heights, Ohio, which may seem worlds apart from the life I've built in the Washington, D.C., area. But the truth is that my early years prepared me well. My dad was an immigrant cabdriver, and my mom, who hadn't finished college, worked in a department store. My parents impressed upon my brothers and me that no place in the world offered more opportunity than America.

I patched together government grants, loans, and scholarships to go to the University of Cincinnati. I got a great taste of politics as an intern for the Cincinnati City Council (which had an aspiring young member named Jerry Springer), where I had the opportunity to do things like write speeches. I was hooked from the first time I heard my words being delivered by a city council member.

It was early 1973, near the end of the Vietnam War. We were just starting to become aware of the benefits of recycling. Cable television was coming into communities, and they had to dig up people's yards to put in the cable. This was a big issue, and so was adding fluoride to the drinking water so kids would have fewer cavities—some people saw this as a Communist plot. I'm almost nostalgic for these issues now.

I chose a graduate school in the Washington, D.C., area, and got a Senate staffer job at age twenty-one. The hardest job to get in politics is the first one, and mine turned out to be life changing. Not only did I gain invaluable experience, I met my future husband, who worked in the same office. Our future was set: living in Washington and working in government.

My career was partially sidelined when our children were born, but I was drawn to continue participating in politics. One day, eight months pregnant and pushing a stroller, I walked into a candidate's office and said, "I want to help. I'm going to be busy in the next few weeks, but I'll be back." Now, twenty-six years later, I have been a local precinct official, county party vice chair and chair, statewide campaign coordinator, and elected DNC member for sixteen years.

Words I live by

On the Margaret Mead quote "Never doubt that a small group of thoughtful, committed citizens can change the world. Indeed, it is the only thing that ever has": This quote is a rallying cry for community activists and has given me hope.

We Can Make a Very Real Difference

Politics has been fun and exciting with unbelievable opportunities. But at the core of it all is a basic recognition that what we do in politics matters. Children having health insurance, seniors being able to afford the prescription drugs they need, efforts to reduce the effects of global warming, and securing a better future for all Americans are a few of the goals we reach for when we dive into the political arena.

Take a Chance

Every woman takes her own personal path. Some are traditional, some have many cul-de-sacs along the way. Going back to college in my thirties for a degree in interior design made me a very untraditional student. It also allowed me to bring a different type of understanding into how offices function and the practical effects of space planning. Being a small-business owner has given me another dimension and enabled me to see business from a different vantage point than most politicians.

Take the chance in life to explore. Take a few turns and see where they lead. Open up to different people and places. I am a stronger and happier person for these opportunities and have been able to give back to my community in ways I had never imagined. It's what my parents taught me: There is opportunity out there—just take the chance!

Never Fear What's Next!

I have always benefited from a new door opening when a door is closed behind me. I urge people not to fear taking that next step, even if you don't know where it leads.

Power Is More Than Strength

Like many women, I do not think in terms of "power"— which is quite different from most men, who have been raised to think it's important to be "strong." I think many of us are more concerned with the power of persuasion. For me, the best kind of power is having the ability to engage people and inspire them to get involved. When I first realized that my words were being listened to and my emails were being read, it was a revelation that made me always try to connect on a personal level, bringing real-life experiences into my political work.

Politics Is About People

The most effective advocacy uses people's real-life stories. These stories can measure whether what you are doing is actually going to make a difference. Lead with your heart, not just your head. If it doesn't feel right, don't do it, no matter how much the statistics or data seem to point you in a direction. Value your instincts.

Technology Leveled the Playing Field

Thirty-five years ago I was an appointment secretary for a U.S. senator. Only women held that type of position. Although I controlled who saw the senator, for how long, and when, I wasn't viewed as professional staff despite the fact that I was in graduate school at the time. Today, that position is called "scheduler" and it is a coveted spot for both men and women. Part of the change in the last decade is that both young men and women have grown up with the ability to type. When I graduated from college, men were discouraged from showing their typing skills except as journalists. Women are much better off today simply because they are not seen as better equipped only for administrative tasks. Technology leveled the playing field.

When Politics Is Personal

The moment I knew that my involvement in government mattered came in 1993 as I walked out of the office of the governor of Maryland. I had been to see him about the lack of breast cancer screening in nursing homes. My mother had lived in a nursing home for several years and never been screened. She died unexpectedly after a mastectomy two weeks after a lump had been manually discovered. Had she been screened earlier, her operation might not have been as complicated and her life might have been prolonged. Governor William Donald Schaefer immediately convened a working task force, and I knew we were on the road to making a difference in these protocols in Maryland. A year later, on Mother's Day, we announced new protocols supported by the State of Maryland and the Maryland nursing home industry.

POWER DRESSING

The scrutiny of women's clothing choices in politics is ridiculous. There's definitely a double standard in the ways men and women are judged on appearance. I choose clothes that are comfortable and have a distinct personality, either through color or style. My most important "accessory" is my hair. I have had a silver streak since I was in my early thirties, and it sets me apart more than any piece of clothing ever will. My hair gives me confidence—partly because it shows my confidence in being who I am.

My words for young women

Focus on your own responsibilities and on being a team player, rather than comparing yourself with others and trying to stand out. Do well by doing good, and just keep it simple: Don't overanalyze and complicate things unnecessarily.

A Network of Girlfriends

Loretta Sanchez

Congresswoman (D), 47th district of California ·
First Mexican-American to represent Orange County
in Congress · Second-ranking Democrat on the Homeland
Security Committee · Senior member, Armed Services
Committee · Her younger sister, Linda, was elected in 2002
to represent California's 39th district, making them the first
pair of sisters to serve simultaneously in Congress

We're Growing Our Network, and We Need You

The women in Congress are a network of girlfriends. I'm always excited to see them and hear them speak. For so many years, Congress was an old-boys' network. I don't know whether young women today are familiar with that term, but that old-boys' club really exists, and when I got into politics twelve years ago, it was going strong.

Now women are creating a counterbalance and growing our network of girlfriends. We have to do this if we want to get into office and be effective there. By the way, *office* means "management of power," because when you hold an office, you get to make decisions about how tax dollars are spent. It's all about power and money, whether you're on the city council or the school board, or in state government or the U.S. Congress.

Life Is Not a Fairy Tale, and That Prince Ain't Coming

We women are still taught not to ask about power or even think about it. We're taught: Don't ask about finances. Someone is going to take care of you. We learn the Cinderella story and the Sleeping Beauty story, where looking good will get us the prince on his white horse. Then we'll be swept off our feet and live happily ever after—whatever that means. This is what we were taught when I was young. Maybe things have changed, but I don't think they've changed that much. (Sometimes when things get really tough, I think to myself, *Where is that guy on the white stallion? Because I could sure use him now.*)

Guys are taught differently. They're taught that power is good. They're taught that they are heroes, that they can run companies, that they can be president. So when there's an opening in Congress, the assumption among guys is that it's going to be filled by a guy. And believe it or not, the assumption is the same among women, because that's the way it's always been.

So when candidates are recruited to fill that opening in Congress, the guys look at who is serving at the state or local level to see if any of their friends are there, so they can help move them up. This is how men think. We need to do the same. We need to recruit our girlfriends who are serving in state governments and city councils, and help get them into the House.

Step Out from Behind the Scenes

House Speaker Nancy Pelosi didn't see herself as speaker when she first ran for Congress. Nancy is one of the most powerful women in the world, and her colleagues had to talk her into her running for leadership. We had to paint the picture for her. She's seen how women have had to struggle to get elected; we've all seen it. Now my colleagues and I—my girlfriends and I—are here to encourage you to claim those positions of power because we need you there.

If you look at any political campaign, who is doing the work? It's not the male candidate. It's his wife who's raising the money, throwing the fund-raising events. It's the women behind the scenes. Do you think that guys know how to plan a party or reception? Book the venue? Plan the menu? Keep it under budget? Do you think they can manage these details? No. They ask the women to put it together. Women are doing the work to get men elected. We need to get *ourselves* elected.

I have a good friend in Congress who was elected at age twenty-five. He went from college to law school to running for Congress. His daddy had been a congressman in the same seat—you get the picture. He came to me as a new congressperson and said, "I need you to help me get a seat on the Ways and Means Committee." That's the taxation committee. I looked at him and started laughing. I said, "You've never even *been* taxed, because you've never worked, so you've never earned a paycheck. Why should you be the one taxing other people's hard-earned money?"

First Things First: Be the Best You Can Be

Do you see what I'm saying? Your life experience counts for something. Whatever job you do, do it well, and then run for office. When people ask you what experience you've had, tell them, "I was the best teacher in that classroom. And let me tell you where my students went to college after they finished with me." If you're good at your job in a measurable way, you have something concrete to tell people—something to sell. I recommend that you volunteer on campaigns first to see whether you like the work. You have to like raising money to be a politician. You have to like going from door to door. You have to like *people.* And you have to be passionate about an issue.

The Value of a Female Perspective

Women bring a unique perspective to government. Nancy Pelosi is a good example. During the war in Kosovo, she was an appropriator on the Foreign Affairs Committee. We were appropriating billions of dollars for the reconstruction of Kosovo, and Nancy inquired about the women who had been abused and raped during the conflict. She wanted to know what happened to these women. She understood that if you don't fix the woman, you don't have a family unit. If you don't have a good family unit, you'll never develop a vibrant society.

Women understand the importance of healthy families. If Nancy hadn't been there and understood that, we wouldn't have been able to offer real help. This is why it's so important for women to be in positions of power and money—and why it matters so much that women aspire to be president.

Be True to Yourself, Even If It Gets You in Trouble

Don't let the system change you. When I first ran for Congress, my husband and I had dinner with some consultants to discuss strategy. One topic I remember vividly was my image: They wanted to frump me up. My husband looked over at them and said, "I don't want a Stepford wife." I naturally disagreed with them as well. First and foremost, I'm a Californian, and I can't hide that! I'm different. Sometimes I get in trouble for it. Some people think I'm too sexy, too spicy, too open . . . too direct. But that works for me. Many women think they have to change their style because it's easier to blend in. But I say, choose to be who you are.

POWER DRESSING

I'm sure if I decided to run for president, people would say, "She's the *Playboy* congresswoman. She shows cleavage on the House floor!" You'd be

amazed at the calls we get when I wear something
a little bit low cut. But I'm not going to be a
frump. I don't wear flip-flops. I don't wear a bikini
on the house floor. I know what's decent and
what's not. I had a good mom who taught me that.

My words for young women

Before you run for office at any level, do something
you're passionate about. If you're a teacher, be the
best teacher there is. If you're a janitor, be the best
janitor there is. But be something, be somebody
before you ask people to support you.

What Women Don't Know

Fran Drescher

Film and television actress and comedian · Rape and cancer
survivor · Public diplomacy envoy, Women's Health Issues
for the U.S. State Department · Women's health activist and
founder of the Cancer Schmancer Movement · Author of
Enter Whining and *Cancer Schmancer*

Life Certainly Is Full of Surprises

I was a chubby kid from Queens raised in a humble
home by working-class parents. Somewhere along the
line I moved to California, married my high school
sweetheart, survived being raped at gunpoint, became a
famous TV star, divorced my high school sweetheart,
lost the TV show, fell in love again, survived cancer, and
reinvented myself as a women's health advocate and U.S.
diplomat. Whose life is that, anyway? I *still* can't believe
it's mine.

Once I was on a flight to Paris and found myself
seated next to the president of CBS. I quickly ran to the
bathroom to put on some makeup, and used the next
several hours to convince him to let me pitch my ideas

for my own show when we were back in Los Angeles. (Where was he gonna go? Coach?) That's how *The Nanny* was born.

Overnight, my dreams of fame and fortune materialized. I was the star of a hit television series. But that's not the end of the story. As *The Nanny* progressed, my marriage was falling apart, and during the last year of filming I began experiencing unusual symptoms. I knew something was wrong.

I was diagnosed with early menopause, but that didn't sit well with me. I felt sexy, young, and on top of my game. I went to specialist after specialist; I got in the stirrups more times than Roy Rogers. Finally, after two years and eight doctors I was diagnosed with uterine cancer. *Oy vey*, this was a lulu! I mean, it really leveled me to the ground, and from that point life for me would be divided into B.C. and A.C.: before cancer and after cancer.

I realized that although I have always been an "alpha" woman, a leader, the one who supported everyone else, the smartest thing to do when I was diagnosed with cancer was to let my friends and family support me. I had to lean on them. I couldn't have made it through without them. After all my expensive therapy, the cancer was my opportunity to put what I had learned into practice. There's no shame in asking for help or being vulnerable.

Words I live by

"No pessimist ever discovered the secrets of the stars, or sailed to an uncharted land, or opened a new heaven to the human spirit."

—HELEN KELLER

Women Needed a Voice, and I Was It

The cure for my cancer was a radical hysterectomy, a difficult operation for any woman, but for one like me who had never had children, it was a particularly bitter pill to swallow. I couldn't wrap my mind around the fact that I would never give birth to a child. The cure seemed like a punishment on a punishment. But in my never-ending quest to turn lemons into lemonade, I turned my experience into a *New York Times* best seller called *Cancer Schmancer.*

When I went on my book tour, thousands of people had similar tales of misdiagnosis and mistreatment. Women wanted to follow me in my quest to challenge authority and change our health system. They needed a voice, and I was it.

So I went to Washington and met with dozens of members of Congress and White House staff. I told them that what women don't know is killing us. And it worked! The bill I was lobbying for, the Gynecologic Cancer Education and Awareness Act (also known as Johanna's Law), passed by unanimous consent, and President Bush signed it into law. It was the first bill of its kind in U.S. history, and allocated millions of dollars to educate women about the earliest warning whispers of women's cancers.

With that victory behind me, I launched the Cancer Schmancer Movement, dedicated to ensuring that all women with cancer are diagnosed in stage 1 when it is most curable. I began spending less time acting and more time advocating. My role as a women's health advocate has taken me around the globe and has enriched my life in so many ways. Sometimes the best gifts come in the ugliest packages.

We all make plans for what we think our future will be, but no one has a crystal ball. And one Wednesday afternoon, should you get sideswiped and your life changes forever, it's time to let go of the old plan, and play a new one. That was a great life lesson for me, a true silver lining, because it taught me to live in the moment as all the great Zen masters teach.

An Unconventional Path to Politics

The new and improved, live-in-the-moment Fran found myself in Washington one afternoon meeting with First Lady Laura Bush's staff. I said, "Lame duck, schmame duck—I need to share my message with women around the world!" Before I knew it I had been appointed a Public Diplomacy Envoy by the U.S. State Department. I continue to travel on behalf of the U.S. government, speaking to women everywhere about taking control of our bodies.

The woman is the caregiver to the child, the spouse, and the elders in almost every home worldwide. At all costs, she must keep herself alive. She is the glue that holds family together and is every nation's greatest natural resource.

In addition to my role as a nonpartisan women's health advocate and diplomacy envoy, I am passionate about advancing progressive causes such as implementing universal health care, creating female-friendly societies, modernizing education for our children, protecting the environment, and defending liberty and justice for all. So I signed on as a surrogate to help Hillary Clinton in her bid to become the first woman president. After her history-making campaign drew to a close, I called Barack Obama and said, "I'm all yours, baby! Consider me an Obama mama!"

When Women Vote, Women Win

When women are empowered with knowledge, we're unstoppable. We need to lock elbows and become one collective voice in order to see real change. We are all women living in a man's world, and that commonality must override political and religious differences if we ever hope to shift that paradigm.

So when you finish reading this book, put it down and go do something! Open your mouth; start a petition. This is your government and your world. Make sure your voice is heard, and make sure you vote, because when women vote, women win. To quote Frederick Douglass, a great American, "Power concedes nothing without demand. It never has, and it never will."

Tried and True Wisdom

The best recipe in life is to turn lemons into lemonade.

What One Woman Can Do

I want to create a more child-, female-, and eco-friendly society. My goals have become more focused on health and education because, to quote first-century B.C.E. writer Publilius Syrus, "Good health and good sense are two of life's greatest blessings."

Advice from a Higher Power

"Know before whom you stand." This quote from the Talmud says it all.

POWER DRESSING

Yes, women's wardrobes are scrutinized more than men's, but *Whattayagonnado*? I like a stunning skirt suit that's nicely tapered, shows off the butt, and a nice pair of heels!

My words for young women

Don't try and emulate a man. Be a woman; it's your greatest strength.

Daughter of Two Cultures

Maria Teresa Petersen

Founding executive director, Voto Latino

The Accidental Advocate

I was an immigrant kid from Bogotá, Colombia, and grew up in rural Sonoma, California. As far as my parents were concerned, my destined path was to become a doctor, accountant, or lawyer—ideally, all three professions, though they'd have settled for any one of them. As most first-generation children know, these are all respectable degrees that catapult you into a new socioeconomic class and guarantee financial security. Let's just say that my parents' dreams went unfulfilled and that they do not quite understand my work today—but they do respect it.

From an early age, I dedicated myself to public policy and social advocacy. My parents scratch their heads, wondering where my social activist streak comes from, but I know. My childhood formed my outlook, my sense of justice, my determination to battle stereotypes, and my skills in the fine art of negotiation.

My father and mother met around my first birthday. My biological father walked out on my mother shortly after my birth, and my mother found herself struggling financially, living with her mother and five younger sisters in a cramped apartment. Unlike the United States, Colombia did not have a safety net for young single mothers. There was no welfare, no job training, no food stamps, no prenatal care. Colombia was a kind of ground zero for Darwin's "survival of the fittest" theory.

Motherhood caught my mother by surprise. Although she'd had vocational training in accounting, her chances of breaking out of the cycle of poverty were slim. Poverty studies confirm that had we stayed in Colombia, my own path of possibility would not have strayed far from hers.

My father, an English teacher, fell in love when he met my mother. About three years into their courtship, he underwent brain surgery for encephalitis, and his doctors ordered him to return home to the States to recuperate. We landed in my grandparents' house in Geyersville, California, a small town of about 3,000 people segregated into two groups: white farmers and Mexican migrant field hands. My grandparents, who were grape growers, disapproved of my parents' relationship both because my mother had a child from a previous relationship and because she was Latina. They made their disapproval clear. While my father got nursed back to health, my mother worked in my grandparents' fields and cleaned my grandmother's friends' homes to sustain the three of us. My extended family became a microcosm of American race relations as we battled our own perceptions and sought to understand each other.

Growing up between two cultures, battling ethnic stereotypes, and being acutely aware of how limited my opportunities would have been had I grown up in Colombia, I developed a strong sense of justice and a deep passion for fulfilling America's promise of self-determination. I draw on my early childhood experience to help me figure out the best ways to have a positive impact on the fastest-growing segment of Americans.

Harnessing the Power of the Next Generation

According to a January 2009 *Newsweek* poll, for every death in the United States, eight Americans of Latino descent are born. Immigration is no longer the influx of Latinos, but the children of those immigrants. If we want a sound, prospering nation, we need to work collectively to ensure that this population is healthy, educated, and economically robust, because now, by and large, it's not.

As a first-generation Latina who translated American cultural norms for my family, I knew that my experience was not unique, and that there were other young people like me who could become a powerful force for change. So I embarked on the work of transforming Voto Latino from a simple public service announcement campaign in 2004 into a full-fledged organization that leveraged new media, the latest technology and celebrity spokespeople to get out the Latino vote. Most critically, Voto Latino relies on acculturated Latinos like me who love America, and on other Americans who see the need to enfranchise this slice of our nation.

America, as conceptualized by our forefathers, is an evolving democracy that is constantly tested in order to grow stronger. The women's suffrage movement of the early 1900s was one such test; the Civil Rights movement of the 1960s was another. Today, as America continues to fulfill our forefathers' dream of equality and self-determination, incorporating Latinos into America's fabric is the foremost challenge of my generation.

Today, Latinos are at the bottom rung of the ladder when it comes to education, health care, and mental health. Our rates of incarceration compete with those of African-Americans. One way Latinos can work toward improving their quality of life is by understanding the electoral process and ensuring that they elect leaders with their best interests in mind.

The Latino population is growing exponentially. Ensuring that this group understands how to navigate the political process should be a priority not just for Latinos but for all Americans. If we fail to have an educated, healthy, and economically sound American Latino population, our parents and children will bear the brunt of that failure.

Be Part of Something Bigger

My childhood experiences of battling stereotypes, negotiating fair treatment, and believing in America's offerings have helped me understand the dynamics of power. I have learned that power is not about an individual. In fact, there is a limit to what one person can do to tackle our large-scale problems such as poverty, racism, and other social inequities. Power is about motivating and organizing a community and working jointly to address these issues. Regardless of our backgrounds, educational attainment, and wealth, we all have the choice to be part of larger movements to improve our communities and our neighborhoods. Each of us has a vested interest in the success of our policies.

Use the Tools at Your Disposal

I'm part of SheSource, the database of female experts offered by the Women's Media Center. I've made a lot of media appearances, and more than once I've had the opportunity to go up against Chris Matthews on *Hardball*. You don't realize the importance of the media until you're there and start making your case and changing the dialogue—and people start caring.

What Do You Mean, I Can't Be President?

I came here from Colombia when I was four, at a time when Colombia had a lot of violence, a lot of exiles. I went to a Catholic school, and I remember one day when I was nine years old, our teacher asked us what we were thankful for. I raised my hand and said, "I'm thankful because yesterday I became an American citizen." No one else knew what that meant, but I had an idea because I remembered what Colombia was like. You'd step out of your house to go to the grocery store and not be sure if you were going to be able to come back.

I wasn't raised to be political, but I was, even then. One day I came home crying from fourth grade. My father asked, "What's wrong?"

I sobbed, "I thought the United States was the land of possibility. But I just learned that I can't be president because I wasn't born here. I don't know what I'm going to do."

My father just looked at me and said, "I can't relate to you right now."

It got worse. The following year we were invited to our neighbors' house for Thanksgiving, and all of a sudden I started talking about what was wrong with Reaganomics. After that, we were banned from their Thanksgiving table. They told my parents, "We think you're lovely, but you can't bring your daughter."

My family's still trying to figure out exactly what I do. I have my master's from the Kennedy School of Government at Harvard, but when I go home for Thanksgiving, I have to tell my relatives I have a doctorate. They understand what a doctor or a lawyer or an accountant is, but they think a master's doesn't count.

My words for young women

Know who your friends are, and keep them close. Success—every kind of success—is about making sure you build relationships. That's the best piece of advice I can share.

What Will You Do to Keep Us Safe?

Kay Granger

Congresswoman (R), 12th district of Texas · First woman on the Defense Appropriations Subcommittee · Ranking member, State/Foreign Operations Subcommittee · Former mayor, Fort Worth, Texas

Playing It Safe Never Gets You There

I was a girl of modest means and modest ambitions. I worked hard in school, prepared to be a teacher (as my mother was), and expected to marry, have children, and reach my ambitions in education.

Then, as they say, life happened.

I was a high school teacher with three children under age three when my marriage ended. I quickly found that while my salary worked fine as a second income, it was nowhere near enough to give me or my children the life I had expected. So I quit teaching and introduced myself to the business world. I sold insurance during the day, studied and prepared at night after I had put the children to bed, and prayed a lot. I was on commission: No sales, no income. That will make or break you in a hurry.

My modest girlhood ambitions disappeared and my life plans went into overdrive. I soon opened my own agency and got involved in local politics. I began to take positions on boards and commissions, and then I ran successfully for the city council. Two years later, I was elected mayor of Fort Worth, and after three terms as mayor, I went on to the U.S. Congress.

Along my journey I often thought of my mother. Despite the limitations her generation faced, she achieved much. She inspired students, taught them about life and learning, and was remembered as their favorite teacher. She became a principal and an administrator. She served on the school board after her retirement, and her proudest achievement was having a school named for her.

But I was moving ahead in my life so quickly and with such determination that I seldom focused on what the women of her generation had done to pave the way for women like me. That was the way it was—until I worked with the women of Iraq.

Words I live by

"Well-behaved women seldom make history."
　　　　　　　—Laurel Thatcher Ulrich,
Harvard professor and historian of early
America and the history of women

A Lesson in Courage

After the United States toppled Saddam Hussein's regime, the Iraqi people prepared for their first free and open election in nearly thirty years. They had written into law that one-third of all who were elected to their parliament and to write their constitution would be women. Within one election, Iraq would have twice the percentage of women in its parliament as we had in our Congress!

I was asked to take a delegation of members of Congress to Iraq to meet with the Iraqi women who were running for office to offer help and encouragement. There I found some of the most courageous women I have ever met. The experience left me with a deepened commitment to paying my dues in the world for the opportunities I have as an American woman in the twenty-first century.

There they were, all in one room—Shias, Sunnis, Kurds, Christians—women completely swathed in black, only their eyes showing. Sophisticated women, highly educated, speaking four and five languages. Young women. Old women. Women who had traveled outside their villages for the first time in their lives. Women who had lived abroad and doubted our motives. Women who were urgently anxious to tell their stories and be heard and understood.

They had traveled as long as thirteen hours to come to this meeting, with bodyguards. Because they were educated and accomplished, their lives and the lives of those around them were at risk. They had been questioned, and some had been shot at. They came to tell us their hopes and fears. They wanted desperately to believe we would listen. They feared we would not understand. Yet slowly, we did understand. We understood what hopes they had for their country and the upcoming election. The meeting took on an urgency and seriousness that could not be denied or choreographed. No town hall meeting could compare with this. No political consultant could prepare these talking points.

The women's stories were horrifying in their brutality. They told their reasons for taking this dangerous step to meet with us, and impressed upon us their love of country and hopes for stability. They asked us to go back to Washington, tell their stories, and ask for additional security through this election. We promised we would. When we returned home, after that trip and the ones that followed, we spoke for the women of Iraq.

Those of us who took on this grave responsibility were forever changed. Freedom to us was something we took with such certainty. A threat to us might have been career limitations—not having our families killed in their homes. One eloquent woman said to me, "Congresswoman, I have read your biography. You have three children almost the exact age of mine. Mine, too, live in the United States. They live there because of the danger here. My children have begged me to take my name off the ballot. They have told me that running for office here will mean I will not live to see my grandchildren. My son was kidnapped. My family's lives have all been threatened. What will you do to keep us safe? What will you do to protect us in this election?"

She poured out her concerns until I finally asked her, "Why are you doing this? How can you be so brave? How can you risk your life and the lives of your family?"

"To have the possibility of having what you have had, Congresswoman Granger," she replied. "To have in this country what you, the women of the United States, have in your lives and in the lives of your daughters."

What Power Has Meant to Me

I never sought power. I sought solutions. I saw problems that needed to be solved, issues that needed resolution. The power I gained came as a surprise, and it came rather quickly. What I didn't know served me well. I didn't know you were supposed to just listen for a while, get the "lay of the land," keep your mouth shut. I dived right in, brought people together, and took control. What I found most helpful, and what women do instinctively, was to bring people along.

When I began my career, I was often the only woman I encountered in my business, and on the boards and commissions I served on. So I didn't have many women leaders to learn from. I became mayor when the five largest cities in Texas were all headed by women, and Ann Richards was governor. Because of this unique situation, we all received a lot of media attention and I began to read about how women lead. It was then that I began to see the differences in how we use power and how we make decisions. Women lead inclusively, not exclusively, so that the solution comes by getting others to buy into your program. We are much more win/win than male leaders.

You Can't Do It All Well All the Time

I was a single parent who owned a business and served in public office. Some days I was a great mother; some days I was a very savvy businesswoman; some days I was a brilliant mayor: I can't remember a single day when I was all three at the same time. One has to make choices and sacrifices. Just make sure they are worth it and do your best. My sons can iron and cook. My daughter can fix anything. They are all very independent, successful adults.

Don't Try to Be "One of the Boys"

Women have incredible strengths. At a time when we are facing enormous challenges in the nation and in the world, the ability of women to bring people together and seek long-term solutions is increasingly important. Most women, given a job to do, do not focus on what title, office space, or salary they will be given. Women focus on doing the job exceptionally well. We can think outside the box because we were excluded from making the box to begin with.

"What Are We Gonna Do with Her?"

When I was mayor, I was helping to deliver meals-on-wheels, and we walked into the house of a ninety-year-old

man. My escort said, "Mr. Smith, this is Mayor Granger."
He glanced at me and looked away. She said again, "This
is the mayor." And he said, "But she's a woman. What are
we gonna do with her?" I've always remembered that because times have changed so much. There are more of us
in office. We are no longer given assignments based on
"women's issues." I was the first woman ever to be chosen
to serve on the Defense Subcommittee of Appropriations.
I am now the ranking member on the State and Foreign
Operations Subcommittee, serving alongside Nita Lowey.
Those are not positions that would ever have been assigned
to women a short time ago.

I Know Just from the Look on Their Faces

My mother was the most powerful influence on my life.
She was the oldest in her family when her father left and
her mother had a mental breakdown. At age fifteen, she
took over the family, began teaching, and bought them a
home. When I was a child, she had a severe case of polio.
After months in the hospital, she returned to teaching on
crutches. She spent two years in physical therapy and
lived with pain the rest of her life. She and my father divorced when I was a teenager. She continued to teach and
to further her career. She attended school at night, gain-
ing her master's degree and several important certifi-
cations. My mother then became the first woman to be
appointed principal of a secondary school. The year after
she retired, she was elected to the school board with enormous community support. To this day, people approach

me and just from the look on their faces, I can see that they are going to tell me a story about how this remarkable woman influenced their lives.

The Bravest Women

The Iraqi women we met with put themselves in enormous danger by involving themselves in their country's first election after Saddam Hussein. Several were killed, and many had family members killed. Nearly half had exiled themselves from Iraq because they were educated and had careers. They returned because of the enormous opportunity to turn their country around and offer opportunities for women in Iraq again. I helped form an Iraqi Women's Caucus in Congress, and we hosted six delegations from Iraq. We mentored them through the elections and the writing of their constitution. They are the bravest women I have ever known. I came away from that experience with a renewed appreciation for the enormous freedom and opportunity we have in this country, and a renewed commitment to protect it.

POWER DRESSING

A red suit. When I was mayor of Fort Worth, I invited Governor Ann Richards to give a major address. I greeted her at a private reception with the city's twenty-five top business leaders. I was dressed in a navy blue suit that I thought was both tasteful and powerful. The first thing

Governor Richards said to me was, "Don't ever wear that suit again." I was crushed. She told me to look around—a roomful of men in navy blue suits! "Part of the power women have," she explained, "is to be the center of attention, in red, yellow, orange, purple. The cameras will go right to us." The next time I saw her was in Washington at the inaugural ball. She was wearing an orange dress with sparkles. The cameras were all on her. I haven't owned a blue suit since.

My words for young women

When it comes to power, being safe never gets you where you want to be. I want women to take chances, to put themselves in positions where they will not be comfortable. Women too often feel they have to overly prepare, control the situation, and perform perfectly. I have found my most satisfying challenges are the ones where I have done just the opposite. I go for a position that makes me stretch—intellectually, emotionally, and physically. That's how to grow.

Why Not You?

Jan Schakowsky

Congresswoman (D), 9th district of Illinois ·
Member, Energy and Commerce Committee

Don't Wait to Be Asked

Brown University once did a study to find out why more
women don't run for office—because when women do run,
they win in the same percentages that men do. The re-
searchers surveyed a thousand men and a thousand women
from the worlds of business, law, education. One question
they were asked was, "Are you qualified to run for office?" Women were *twice* as likely as men to say no—that
they were not qualified to run. This was even true of the
younger women, and that really surprised me. I thought
we would find a dramatic difference in women who'd
grown up in a more open, feminist environment.

But that study also found that one of the predictors of
whether somebody runs for office is if they're *asked* to
run. So everywhere I go now, I ask women to at least think
about running—just as I was asked. I was already in my

forties when I ran my first race. But I'd been an activist for years.

I was born in 1944 in the district I represent. My neighborhood, Rogers Park in Chicago, was primarily Jewish then. My mother, a teacher, was born in Canada, her parents' first stop before coming to Chicago from Russia, and my father, a furniture salesman, was born in Russia, making me a first-generation American. I received a degree in elementary education from the University of Illinois, got married, taught for a couple of years, and then "retired" to raise my children.

Words I live by

"Never doubt that a small group of thoughtful,
committed citizens can change the world.
Indeed, it's the only thing that ever has."
—MARGARET MEAD

Six Housewives on a Mission

My political career started in 1969, though I wouldn't know that for more than a decade. A small group of suburban housewives—six of us—got together to demand to be told the age of the food we were purchasing in the grocery store. We (modestly) called ourselves National Consumers United.

Back then, nobody knew whether the foods on grocery store shelves were fresh. Everything was code dated with numbers, letters, and colors. We cracked those codes by getting the stock boys—who rotated the food on the shelves, putting the oldest in front—to tell us how they knew which products were older. We published those codes in a book that sold 25,000 copies.

We conducted store inspections and found food that was days, weeks, months, and years beyond the date the manufacturers believed to be fresh enough to sell, and removed those products from the shelves. Baby food and infant formula were often the most out of date. We became shareholders (one share) in the Jewel supermarket chain and National Tea Company, and wrote dense, single-spaced press releases about our efforts.

We won! Jewel began to advertise "freshness dates," and Oscar Mayer, a big offender, put clear expiration dates on their packages. For a twenty-five-year-old stay-at-home mom, this was an exhilarating and empowering experience, transforming me from an ordinary housewife to an ordinary housewife who could make a difference in the world.

Why Not Run for Office?

That experience led me to other organizing and advocacy efforts, and eventually to such jobs as executive director of the Illinois State Council of Senior Citizens. In 1986, my girlfriends said, "Why don't you run for the Cook County Board in the Chicago area?" And I said, "Why not?"

I remember that first campaign. You have to meet and greet lots of people, and my first stop was the Greek church picnic. I thought, *Oh my God, it's the middle of summer. The election isn't until November. If I go into the food tent where families are eating and talk about politics, won't they tell me to just go home?* But it didn't take me long to realize that most people are nice. Or polite, at least. Most people are, in fact, impressed. They'll think, *Oh, you're a politician? You're running for office? You're important. And you want to shake my hand? That's a good thing.*

That was a revelation. It made me more confident about knocking on doors or asking for money. I lost my first race; none of the Democrats won that year. But I learned a lot, including that I really enjoyed campaigning. I built a reputation and, even more important, a list of supporters and contributors. When my state representative decided to run for higher office in 1990, I immediately jumped into the race, and after a challenging primary and general election, I won. I served in the Illinois General Assembly for eight years, continuing my work as a consumer and health care advocate.

In 1998 my congressman decided to retire after fifty years in elective office. It was a solidly Democratic district, and I knew that whoever won the primary could likely serve for many years. There was a very competitive primary in which I ran against a billionaire and a veteran senator. I built a strong grassroots campaign, engaging young people from across the country to come to Chicago and work as organizers. I also raised a greater percentage of money from women than any other federal candidate. It was an exciting and successful race.

A decade later, I still feel incredibly privileged to represent my diverse, progressive district, and I continue my consumer advocacy, now as a part of the Democratic leadership of the House. As vice chair of the Subcommittee on Commerce, Trade, and Consumer Protection, I played a leading role in passing the most sweeping reforms to consumer product safety laws in a generation. As Democratic co-chair of the bipartisan Women's Caucus in the House for the 111th Congress, I will be leading efforts to improve the lives of women around the world.

Hey, I'm Your Representative. I Could Change Your Life.

Every election cycle, I stand out in front of the El (Chicago's mass transit system) and try to meet as many people as possible. Sometimes a young person makes a wide swath around me and says, "I'm not interested." If I had more time, I'd say, "Come back and talk to me about what part of your life you're not interested in." Because I may be the vote that decides if a young woman is forced to carry a pregnancy to term. I may be the person who decides whether or not college loans are available.

It's so important that we have a greater balance of women in politics. Even today, we bring a different life experience to the table. Government works best when all life experiences are part of the debate before policies are set. When there were no women in Congress, for example, all the clinical studies on heart disease were done on men. But when women got elected, we started asking why studies were not being done on women—and when those studies were done, they found significant differences in heart disease between the sexes.

This is a historic moment in U.S. history. I have never been as optimistic, despite all the economic and foreign policy challenges our country faces, that our government and our leaders, of which I am one, will be able to play a significant role in making people's lives better, helping to save our planet from the ravages of global warming, and building a more peaceful world. I urge all young women to think about making the journey into a political life. There are still a lot of doors to open and ceilings to crash through. But if we are going to make the kind of changes we really need in this world, we have to do it.

My Lightbulb Moment

Before I held office, I had been working for various progressive advocacy organizations, trying to pass state legislation on issues like affordable health care, energy policy, and job creation. It wasn't long before I realized that I was as smart and qualified as the people I was lobbying. That's when I started thinking about running for office myself.

Keep Looking for "Yes"

In politics, you will hear "No" from strangers and even friends when you call on them for support or money. Count on it. The secret is to just keep looking for "Yes," not focusing on that "No," and certainly not taking it as a personal rejection. It's a skill you learn—not to feel bruised and battered when you step out. There are a whole lot of reasons why people may turn off to you, and your job is to figure out what they're looking for. If you stay true to yourself and your mission, you will learn to take the blows and not feel defeated. They come with the territory. If you need everyone to like you, choose another profession.

Sometimes Adequate Is Good Enough

Don't judge yourself against perfection. Be kind to yourself. Sometimes adequate is good enough. I used to obsess about the one small mistake I made in a speech, rather than the fact that people had appreciated what I had to say. Watch how men are able to fall on their faces, get up, dust themselves off, and keep going. Even if you are nervous—voice shaking, knees knocking—do what you need to do. Your passion and sincerity will come through, and those are the ingredients that make you compelling and attractive. Before you know it, your voice gets stronger and you feel your own power.

Now Little Girls Can Dream of Different Things

I was at the 1984 convention at which Geraldine Ferraro was nominated for vice president. At one event I attended, Walter Mondale, the presidential candidate, introduced her and she came out. Suddenly I found myself crying—really crying. Then I glanced around the room, which was full of women of all ages. There was not a dry eye in that room. We all knew that something important had happened. We were just so proud that little girls could dream about different things. When I was growing up, the options were quite limited. It was pretty much nurse or teacher—I became a teacher like my mother. Of course there were ground-breaking women who went into law and business and all kinds of fields that were untraditional at the time. It's remarkable to me that we're still ticking off "firsts."

POWER DRESSING

I call it looking "candidential." Mostly it means looking put together and professional. That leaves room for lots of different styles: pantsuits, like Hillary Clinton's; interesting and colorful fashions like Congresswoman Rosa Delauro's; business suits, skirts of all lengths—except too short. The idea is to dress in a way that makes the statement you want to make about yourself, and not to put off the people you're trying to engage. Yes, women are more scrutinized than men, but that's just a fact one learns to deal with. I have tried to make it a plus. I have a red coat for every season. Occasionally it's referred to in the press as my "signature" red coat.

My words for young women

Investing in women is the best thing you can do to create a more peaceful, more healthful, more productive society.

Inner Strength Trumps
Outer Strength

Cathy McMorris Rodgers

Congresswoman (R), 5th district of Washington · Member,
House Armed Services, Education and Labor, and Natural
Resources Committees · Vice chair, Republican Leadership
Conference · Co-chair, Congressional Women's Caucus

Don't Wait for Someone Else
to Make a Difference

Growing up on a farm, I never dreamed I would someday
be serving in Congress, and I've met many other members who never thought they'd wind up here either. I have
lived the American dream, starting with my parents'
wish for me to go to college. I was the first in my family
to graduate, and that meant working my way through
school. I saved my money from selling 4-H animals, and
worked at McDonald's. After I graduated, I came back
home and worked on a family friend's campaign for the
state house. I had never been involved in politics before,
but I got excited about the issues. Later, he was appointed to the state senate when our senator retired, and
I was appointed to fill his House seat until the next general election.

It's important to give back to your community, and politics is a way to make a difference—not just to sit around and talk about the problems that face your community or state or country, but to put yourself at the table and to come up with solutions. And it's not a matter of waiting until you're "ready"—old enough, seasoned enough—to run for office. When you show people that you're capable, they'll look to you for the next position or opportunity. I was thirty-five when I first ran for the U.S. Congress, and some questioned my decision, saying I was too young. But sometimes your perceived weaknesses are actually your strengths. I had energy and I was able to appeal to a whole different group of people. I knew I had proven myself in the state legislature, so I just decided I was going to work hard and be the best representative I could be.

When I decided to run for Congress, I was amazed at how many people came together to support me. It wasn't just political allies, the network I had developed over ten years in state office. It was other folks I'd met along the way who were excited about me running. Several of them came out and worked on the campaign. My family and close friends stepped up—people who didn't have big bucks but were willing to write bigger checks than they'd probably ever written in their lives because they believed in me.

A Fabulous Time to Be a Woman in Politics

There are 77 women now serving in the House of Representatives—out of 435, so we're right at 17 percent.

That's not a high number, but it is a record, and everyone recognizes that 2008 was quite a year, with Senator Clinton running for president and being appointed secretary of state, and Sarah Palin on the ticket for the Republicans. It's an exciting time for women in politics. It's almost an advantage right now to be female, because people are looking for women to step up and provide leadership. For those of us who are willing to do so, there are tremendous opportunities.

But there are also hurdles, the same ones women have had to jump for years and years. At various times in my career, people have questioned whether I was tough enough. When I was in the Washington State House, I ran for leader of the Republicans—minority leader at that time—and was elected. The main doubt my opponents expressed about my abilities was, Is Cathy too nice? Is she tough enough? Of course that's the same doubt that's often expressed about women in matters of national security. But we are just as tough as men, and we can even be tougher, because inner strength ultimately trumps outward strength. Security is a very important issue for women, though we might not talk about it as much as men do. We're more inclined to talk about health care and education, but protecting our families is right up there on our priorities list. The desire to protect my son from those who want to do him harm is very much a top priority.

You don't have to be a member of Congress to make a difference. People do it day in and day out in their own neighborhoods and cities. They're stepping up to make their communities a better place to live, raise a family, start a small business. That's what the political process is really all about. All it takes to change the world is for us to do our own small part to give back—and to inspire others to want to do the same.

How to Get Your Foot in the Door

Grab the opportunities that come your way, even if they're not what you expected or thought you wanted. Embrace them, and they'll lead to further opportunities. Take advantage of internships in the areas you're interested in pursuing. There are internships in Congress, of course, but also at think tanks, public affairs firms, and nonprofits. Internships can help you see the process from a variety of perspectives and decide where you really want to dedicate your time and energy. If I could do it all over again, I would look for those internships and try to take advantage of them.

My words for young women

It's one thing to talk about solutions. It's another thing to actually bring people together and say, "This is the way forward."

How to Be Yourself
When You Lead

Marie Wilson

President, The White House Project · Co-creator, Take Our
Daughters and Sons to Work Day · Former president, Ms.
Foundation for Women · Author, *Closing the Leadership Gap*

It Started with a Dare

I'm here to recruit you. The most important thing for you,
and for every woman in this country, is to live a deeply
evolved political life.

For many years, I invested myself in the private world
of home and family. My life changed when, on a dare, I
went to New York City to interview for a job heading the
Ms. Foundation for Women. I wasn't looking for a job—in
fact, I had just won a city council position in Des Moines.
But of course, when you aren't really looking for a job,
you're completely irresistible to employers. (Remember
this when you go to an interview: If you pay full attention
to what the organization is and needs, and if you enjoy
the people, they'll come for you.)

I found myself so intrigued by both the mission of the
Ms. Foundation and the passion of people who worked

there that I wound up moving to New York to help build this extraordinary women's organization. After twenty years there, I left to give my full attention to The White House Project, which aims to advance women's leadership in all communities and sectors up to the U.S. presidency.

What made me turn my attention fully to women's political leadership? In essence, young women like you. Over the years I'd been receiving letters from the girls who had gone to work on Take Our Daughters to Work Day, a campaign I helped found. In these letters, girls told me over and over again that they actually wanted to *be* the president one day. *Yikes*, I thought—*we better get cracking at making that possible.*

I was also influenced by looking closely at our Ms. Foundation grantees, and realizing that these women and others like them had been creating the best social policy in the country—while sitting on the outskirts of power. They had created living-wage campaigns and micro-enterprises; they had invented new ways to keep communities safe and deliver health care. And they are still the only people standing between you and a future that doesn't allow you control over your own body.

Looking at all the potential and passion embodied in women and girls across this country, I knew that the next great goal of my life would be to put these women—who I saw as "the government in exile"—into power. I still believe in organizing and advocating for change. But as we do this, we also need to be running for office and claiming that brand of power so we can make the changes permanent.

This "both/and" strategy is one the women's movement has not always fully embraced. But it has always seemed clear to me that you have to work simultaneously at both the top and the bottom of any hierarchy, both inside and outside the system at the same time. You have to get women into leadership in every sector to change the way this country works: from business to media, politics to the military. We need women leading everywhere—and it's going to be up to your generation to make sure this happens.

Words I live by

The first famous woman who inspired me to change my life was Gloria Steinem, who, at the tenth anniversary of the National Women's Political Caucus, wished for all of us to "become the man we wanted to marry." Her words helped me realize how my own dreams had been deferred, and that I was living through my husband's dreams instead. For women of my era, this was expected. But leaving my dreams on the table would have been a mistake, and continuing to burden my husband by living through his dreams was not fair to him either. I think these words continue to be important for young women and young men to hear. We all need to be conscious of when we are sacrificing our dreams, because it can lead to a lifetime of resentment.

Moving Past the Tightrope Dynamic

Only when we get large numbers of women to lead will all women be able to be themselves when they lead. When there's just one woman running or even leading, she inevitably gets caught in the trap of having to prove she's "man enough" for the job, while also maintaining her all-important "likeability." In other words, she has to be both tough *and* feminine at the same time. It's a tricky tightrope to walk—and it was this double bind in particular that became so hard for Hillary Clinton to manage in her campaign.

But it's not just women running for office who face these kinds of challenges. Any woman running for an executive position or leading in a corporate setting has to learn to talk differently, dress differently, empower herself in a different way than she might if she were leading in a field more thoroughly populated by female peers. Women in these situations even have to negotiate differently. They can't be too tough; as author Linda Babcock says, they have to be "relentlessly pleasant" to get what they want. And all these differences—compromises, really—are a direct function of the lack of numbers of women leading at the highest levels.

We can change that dynamic by filling the leadership pipeline with a diverse mass of women who are trained and ready to lead. Because if we keep running one at a time—if there are only eight women governors and eight women CEOs at the top of corporate America—we will always continue to be viewed through the lens of gender, not seen and valued for our agendas. To correct this in the political arena, we may all have to run at once. This may sound funny, but it's already happening: Around the country some women are choosing an issue, such as access to clean water, and running as a team.

Numbers matter—and so do you. In the four years since The White House Project began training women to run for office, nearly 6,000 women have become prepared to run and win. By 2013 we plan to have trained 36,000 more. You must be among them. If it sounds daunting, don't worry: I'll be there to help and cheer you on.

True Friends Will Tell You the Truth— Even If You Don't Want to Hear It

Surround yourself with people you trust who will tell you the truth—including things you don't want to hear. But they also have to let you know they have confidence in you. No matter how strong we are, women get subtle signals daily that they are not trusted. Even for the strongest of us, our confidence can be easily eroded. Finally, you need people around you who trust themselves. That's basic.

Power potholes are also about trust. The failures I have seen women experience in politics and in leadership, including my own, occurred when we gave away power too easily and trusted others too much. Academician Rosabeth Kanter defined another pothole when she wrote about leaders having "pockets of powerlessness." This pothole deepens daily when a leader doesn't have access to the information she needs to lead. Sometimes it's a result of

people trying to "protect" you because they don't understand what you need to hear. Sometimes it's a result of
other people trying to increase their power by withholding
information. I watched a woman who should have been a
governor, and probably a president, fail because people
didn't let information she needed reach her. It was a great
loss to our country.

The Power Pipeline Needs to Lead Somewhere

When I began my career I was living in Iowa, where I was
blessed to witness the leadership of many women who
were courageous and talented legislators. Women in the
West and Midwest have often achieved certain leadership
roles faster than their female peers in other regions because they worked alongside men on farms or ranches
and were seen as tough and able. But what you didn't see
much of were women serving as the heads of these elected
or appointed bodies—as mayors, as school board presidents, or as governors. So while the Midwest had a pipeline with women leaders, it went nowhere. Today, however,
there are examples of women serving in all levels of
government—not enough to make it "normal," but enough
to inspire more women to follow in their footsteps. Additionally, the cabinet appointments of presidents Bill Clinton and George W. Bush—both of whom put more women
in national and international leadership roles—have allowed women to see themselves in high-level positions,
guiding nontraditional issues like national and homeland
security and the economy.

The Ms. President Patch

There were two women who helped me see myself clearly. One was a Christian educator at our church; the other a scout leader. They were both loving and strong and their influence stays with me to this day. In fact, The White House Project developed a Ms. President patch in conjunction with the Girl Scouts to pay homage to scouting as a great training ground for powerful girls and my own history with the organization.

Overcome by Women's Courage

During the 2008 Democratic National Convention, I was overcome by the courage of both Hillary Clinton and Michelle Obama. I grew up in Georgia in the 1940s and 1950s; as a girl, I couldn't have begun to imagine two women leaders like these—women who are different in race, age, and origin, both ensconced as magnificent, eloquent, passionate leaders. I felt grateful that The White House Project had played a small part in readying the country for this moment and for the opportunity we were creating for more women to lead: women who will fight for the issues that will bring other women along. I silently cried my way through the convention, like the tears that come when you listen to beautiful music. Sometimes you have no idea how fast things can change for the better—a comforting thing to remember in hard times.

POWER DRESSING

I love boots. Not up to the knees, but midcalf. They make me feel like I'm supported and a bit tough— even when they're patent leather. A red jacket, a straight-legged pair of pants, and I'm ready to take on whatever comes.

My words for young women

Many of the young women I meet are afraid to admit that they are feminists or to identify with women's issues because they don't want to separate themselves from men. I always remind them that "to be *for* women is not to be *against* men." In fact, it's just the opposite: To be for women is one of the best things you can do for men.

An End to the Insults

Carol Jenkins

President, Women's Media Center ·
Emmy Award–winning former newscaster and correspondent

A Woman's Place Is at the Top

Media is one of the ultimate determining forces in our lives—an instrument of towering power.

What we know, think, and feel about ourselves, our country, and our world is shaped by the messages that bombard us every single day of our lives. Are women as good as men, girls as smart as boys? Is it better to be white or brown, blond or brunette, fat or thin? What do we understand about the impact of joblessness, hunger, homelessness, disease? How do we stop the murderous wars engulfing wide swaths of the world—or do we? How is it possible that women and girls worldwide are raped, blinded, disfigured—and killed—without the rest of the world rising up in protest and action? Is it because the messages we receive discount the value of these girls and women—or because we seldom hear their stories told?

I have worked in the media my entire professional life: as a reporter and anchor, host, producer of documentaries, writer of books; and now, as the head of an organization with the purpose of making sure women and people of color participate fully—and are represented fairly.

People tell me that journalism schools are full of women. They say that when you walk into a newsroom, you see nothing but women. But all those women are working for men. Women hold only 3 percent of the "clout" positions[1]—those at the very top—in media. That means 97 percent of everything we know is, at its highest level, dictated by the male perspective.

Most of the executive suites at the networks and newspapers are full of men. Most of the opinion writers (75 percent of syndicated writers) are men.[2] Some of our most prominent newspapers (*The New York Times, The Washington Post*) have only one or two women columnists on staff—and eighteen or twenty men. On radio, most of the people on the air and behind the scenes (85 percent) are men.[3] Almost all of the directors of major films (96 percent) are men. Most popular Web sites are written by men.[4] Sunday morning interview programs, which dictate "the news" and policy in Washington, are *all* hosted by men. Women and people of color own less than 5 percent of the television and radio stations.[5]

In studies conducted worldwide looking at how many news stories are about women or include women, the figures are an appalling 21 percent.[6]

Women and girls are dying while the cameras are pointed elsewhere.

Words I live by

*"Violence against women is not culture,
it's not custom. It's criminal."*

This powerful quote is from Hillary Clinton, during her confirmation hearings for secretary of state. To have a woman who wields power declare that women in the world matter—and that those who maim and murder young girls and women will not be tolerated—was a thrilling moment.

Make Women Visible

This does not mean that there hasn't been progress. When I began my reporting career in 1970, women were generally restricted to "soft" stories. "Hard" stories were the ones about politics, crime, war, the economy, science, the world—in other words, anything that really mattered. There were no bosses who were women or people of color. Media, this most powerful instrument, was nearly completely staffed by white men.

Today there are respected correspondents, anchors, editors, managers, directors, and heads of studios who are women and people of color. We need to celebrate their success. But you can see from the percentages that there is still much work to be done.

That's why the Women's Media Center was founded in 2006 by activist/writers Gloria Steinem, Jane Fonda, and Robin Morgan. The mission is to make women visible—and powerful—in the media. We're concerned about women media professionals participating in the highest ranks, those "clout" positions, and we want to make sure that the stories of girls' and women's lives are told truthfully and powerfully enough to move the world into action.

We do this in three ways:

First, by advocacy—by pointing out how women are being excluded from the media and how, in some cases, women are still the subject of blatant sexism.

Second, we created a place for women to write. We publish hundreds of commentaries written by women, about women, on our Web site (womensmediacenter.com)—we've created a new, diverse reservoir of writing talent and given women opportunities to build their portfolios.

Finally, we're building a cadre of women experts, training them in media and opinion writing, and actively placing them in a vast array of media opportunities. Our Progressive Women's Voices program trains women to build media plans for themselves or their organizations. Our SheSource database of women experts, with more than 500 of the world's leaders and analysts, is the most comprehensive source available today. Our experts include women who can build nuclear bombs—but would rather talk about eliminating the need for them.

Recently, I found a letter written to me by my very first news director. It said:

Dear Carol,
It has come to our attention that you are attempting to organize the women in the newsroom. Please feel free to leave at any time.

Well, I stayed in the newsroom for over thirty years. Now it's my job to "organize the women." Let's work together to make sure equality doesn't take another thirty years.

The Elements of Power

The acquisition of power is a positive, essential element for making change in the world. But it's long been cast as central to a masculine identity, something for women to reject. As a result, we're still too often beggars for our share.

Master the Details

Whatever the project, complete mastery of the details is essential. We have to approach our work like doctoral candidates: expert at both stating—and defending—our thesis.

Power Is Never Skin Deep

Never let charm replace substance. The insistence that women have to be agreeable and likeable sometimes leads to the assumption that these superficial attributes are all you need.

Beware the Shutout

When I entered the profession of journalism, women and people of color were not permitted to participate. It took riots, federal mandates, and protests by feminists before networks and newspapers let us in. This was not southern segregation—it happened in New York City and across the country. The situation has improved greatly, but women and people of color are still shut out of many major decision-making positions. We've had a woman run for president of the Unites States, putting, as she's said, 18 million cracks in the glass ceiling. That's a crack for each vote she won, and a major achievement, but the ceiling is still there.

Leaving the Farm Behind

When I was growing up, my aunt Minnie was the head of our extended farming family in rural Alabama. She had fourteen brothers and sisters, including my mother, plus some forty-five nephews and nieces. She made sure, with her husband's help, that all eight sisters went to college (she was an early feminist—the boys stayed on to run the farm). Then she saw to it that every one of those nieces and nephews had help going to college. She wielded ultimate power with extremely high expectations. As a result, we did not lose a single person along the way. We grew up with the assumption that we would succeed. And, yes, a lot of lectures.

POWER DRESSING

Looking good is a good thing, but being comfortable in your skin is more important and essential to finding power in your life. I hope I live to see our society reach the point where women don't pay a higher price and face closer scrutiny for our choices of hairstyle and clothes.

NOTES

1. Annenberg Public Policy Center, "The Glass Ceiling Persists," 2003.

2. Media Matters, "Black and White and Re(a)d All Over," 2007.

3. "Women in Media: Facts & Figures," MIW Radio Group, 2006.

4. Salon.com: http://dir.salon.com/story/ent/movies/feature/2002/ 08/27/women_directors/.

5. Free Press, "Off the Dial: Female and Minority Radio Station Ownership in the United States," 2007.

6. The Global Media Monitoring Project: http://www.whomakes thenews.org/images/stories/website/gmmp_reports/top_10_ highlights_2005/top_10_english.pdf.

Wanted: Your Ideas

Marsha Blackburn

Congresswoman (R), 7th district of Tennessee · First woman in Tennessee elected to the U.S. House of Representatives · First woman to represent the 23rd Senate District of Tennessee · Deputy Whip, 110th–111th Congress

Leadership Is a Transferable Commodity

Have you ever had a great idea? Maybe you were listening to the news and thought, *If someone would only do . . . and gee, it wouldn't be hard to make that happen.* Your ideas are needed now. It's a great time for entrepreneurial politics, and that means you need to exercise leadership. You do have leadership skills.

The skills you are developing as you go through life—being part of organizations and clubs—are ones you can bring to the public sector.

Women do that very, very well. When I was running for Congress, I was campaigning in rural Tennessee and I walked into a diner. There was a crusty guy sitting there. I walked over to him and said, "Hi there, sir, I'm State Senator Marsha Blackburn and I'm running for the U.S. House of Representatives. I would appreciate your vote."

I handed him my push card. He took it, turned it over in his hand, and looked at it, and then he looked up at me and said, "Little lady, what qualifies you to run for the U.S. House of Representatives?" I looked back at him and said, "Well, you know what, I've been the three-year-old choir director, the room mother, the room mother chairman, and the Girl Scout cookie mom, and if you can handle those jobs you can handle the U.S. House of Representatives." You know exactly what I'm talking about, don't you?

You are building your ability to lead from real-life, day-to-day experiences that allow you to move forward with confidence. I want you to remember that leadership skills are transferable, and that many women don't walk as traditional a career path as men. We may take time off for children. We may change industries. We may change jobs seven times. It's important for us to realize we're always going to be learning new things to repackage and take with us to new endeavors. We don't have to go back and start over at zero. We just kind of transfer those skills along the way.

Words I live by

"If you want something said, ask a man.
If you want something done, ask a woman."
—MARGARET THATCHER

Leadership Is Not as It Appears, It's as It Performs

You can assign someone a title but you cannot assign action. Action is something you have to *do*, and it's what the American people are hungry for right now. They want people to solve problems, whether it's the problem of taxes, energy, or bureaucracies that don't work. They want action and answers.

In the summer of 2008 I was up in Alaska in the Arctic National Wildlife Refuge, and we were waiting for the fog to lift. I was talking to someone in Barrow about the people who live there. She said, "You know, we've got great leaders here. They're not leaders in the vein that you all in Washington think about leaders." I said, "Well, what kind of leaders are they?"

She said, "They're the kind who throw on the parka, pull on the gloves, and get out there. If something needs to be done they just do it. They take charge and they just get it done." I said, "So it's kind of like Larry the cable guy— just get her done."

She said, "Right. What people want is someone who is going to get in there and take action."

Women are very, very good at that.

This point really hit home when, as a Tennessee state senator, I led a statewide, grass roots effort to defeat a state income tax being proposed by my own party's governor.

Leaders Raise Up Other Leaders

This is very important. Leaders want a deep bench behind them, and you learn better when you teach. You learn better when you mentor. I encourage you to pull someone along with you as you move onto the leadership track and take your position teaching and training others.

In October 2003, I was in Mosul, Iraq, at a women's center. I was talking, the interpreter was translating, and when we got to the word *mentor*, there was no word in their dialect that was a direct translation. So we talked about the concept of how a mentor is more than a teacher, more than a trainer. It's somebody who commits to walk with you and help you become the very best person you can be. Someone does this for you, and you do it for the next person.

One of my inspirations in leadership has been my mother. My mom is eighty-three years old, and in 1997 she won the lifetime achievement award from Keep America Beautiful for her beautification and conservation efforts. She has always said, "First you clean up your home, then you clean up your town, and then you clean up your country." There's a lot of wisdom in that. We can all make certain we are practicing conservation and efficiency to sustain the world around us.

I learned a long time ago, when I was serving in the state senate, that it's a lot easier to do things right the first time: If you can change a piece of legislation, file your amendments, and make sure it's as good as you can get it on the front end, it's going to be better for everyone in general, whether it's the state or the whole country. So, wherever you are, the leadership skills you're developing right now will be useful throughout your whole career— and who knows where you're going to end up using them? I know you'll succeed. My generation expects great things from you.

Focus on What's Important

Women often seek public service to solve problems and right wrongs. Women tend to focus on the big picture and think in terms of the next decade, not the next election. When I first ran for office, I did so because of concern with taxes, small business pressures, and social issues. Today, I keep the focus on faith, family, freedom, hope, and opportunity.

Success Is the Best Revenge

My maternal grandmother, Connie Josephine Meeks Morgan, chose to go to college in the early 1900s and audit agriculture classes because she was not allowed to enroll in them. She became a teacher and didn't marry until she was thirty. She charted her own path and blazed new trails.

Women today will step forward to lead in their own right. They don't wait to be invited. Previously, many of our trailblazers followed successful officeholders who were fathers or spouses. Bias still exists for many women. The way to defeat the bias is to prove you are the best qualified person for the job.

POWER DRESSING

Isn't it odd that in the twenty-first century, some people still focus on this? But it's true that your outer appearance is one element that provides you with the assurance that you are ready, prepared, confident, and competent.

My words for young women

Don't sit back waiting for others to define you—define yourself. Tell your story and your accomplishments.

A From-the-Ground-Up Thing

Shelley Moore Capito

Congresswoman (R), 2nd district of West Virginia · First
Republican woman elected to Congress from West Virginia ·
Member, House Financial Services Committee

My Job Is Not About Me

We now have the greatest number of women serving in
Congress in the history of our country. But if you consider
that Congress has 435 members, we're still very much in
the minority. I'm in my fifth term as the only woman in
West Virginia's congressional delegation. Serving the
people of my state has been, and continues to be, incredibly fulfilling.

I started out as a premed student majoring in zoology.
One summer I worked in a hospital and realized I didn't
have what it took to be a doctor. The sight of blood and
people in pain really were hard for me. I like to joke that
I wound up in Washington, working in the biggest zoo in
America, where everybody's bloodied and in pain.

Actually, I grew up in politics. My father was a six-term
member of Congress and a three-term governor of West

Virginia. I couldn't avoid being involved in his campaigns. He'd say, "Come on, you're going!" and we'd go—to parades, to talk to people, to listen to speeches.

Politics is a from-the-ground-up thing. You can't start as a member of Congress. You've got to start at the city council, the county commission, or as student body president. You start by getting interested in the issues. If you can get an internship in government, it's a great way to get a feel for the lay of the political land and to know what it's really like.

I began my political career as a delegate to the state legislature, and always assumed I would remain in the state house. I never even dreamed about making a run for higher office. I was making a difference in my local community, and that was what mattered.

In 2000 the opportunity to run for Congress presented itself. Instead of thinking of all the reasons why I might not succeed, I mounted what seemed to be an impossible campaign—against a multimillionaire, in a state with an overwhelming Democratic registration advantage. But I'd learned a lot about flexibility and timing as an active mother of three and a local volunteer. And like many women, I had a support system I could count on: fellow parents who sat on the bleachers to watch our kids play sports and friends from local community boards. I looked for every opportunity to meet with voters and constituents. Nothing can substitute for face-to-face interaction with people. I sometimes fantasize that a young girl in the audience might look at me and say, "I want to do that!" What a wonderful legacy that would be!

I won that campaign and became the first Republican woman elected to Congress from West Virginia. It quickly became obvious to me how important a woman's voice can be to the balancing act of Congress. Good policy depends on input from a wide variety of views and perspectives.

People often ask me if it's harder for a woman to get elected, and the answer is no. First of all, whether you're a man or a woman, you have to do your homework. You have to know every side of every issue. That puts you on a level playing field. On that field, being a woman is absolutely an advantage. We project ourselves differently, and our voices are heard in a different way. When we talk about issues, it's from more of a family perspective.

We have a women's caucus in Congress—both Republicans and Democrats—and when we meet, we go right to bipartisan issues where we can find common ground. We explore a lot of international women's issues, such as sexual trafficking or women's and children's health. The caucus also gives us a chance to get together on a more informal basis, without partisanship, and talk about things that are important—not just in our home states but for women in general.

I also started a civility caucus—with my friend Emmanuel Cleaver, a Democrat from Missouri—where both sides could get together and present our platforms in a civil way. We've had debates about taxes, health care, and the War on Terrorism, bearing in mind that we all want to arrive at the same place even if we have different ideas about how to get there.

My job is not about me. It's about what the Second District of West Virginia wants me to advocate for. In the Sago Mine tragedy of 2006, where thirteen miners were trapped, those were my West Virginians and I was there. It was a very sad occasion, and we moved forward in a bipartisan way to develop new safety legislation. There are issues where the two sides disagree because we have a philosophical difference, but there are many more areas where we do agree. In the long run, we work well together.

Today there are women at the very top. Certainly Secretary of State Clinton showed beyond the shadow of a doubt that a woman is qualified, ready, and able to become president of the United States. I believe we're going to see more and more women taking the mantle of power. Still, I'm always mindful of the women who have gone before me. Women like Elizabeth Kee, the first woman elected to Congress from West Virginia, built the foundation that so many modern woman leaders stand on, and I am truly in awe of them. I hope that someday someone may look back at our generation of women leaders and say that we, too, were good stewards of our legacy, that we continued to break down barriers, and that we forged a path for those who follow.

I've always wanted my sons to know strong women because I believe it makes them stronger men. I've always wanted my daughter to know that her future is hers, that she has the power and the freedom to make choices for herself.

The Power in the Process

I ran for office because I wanted to be part of the process to make an actual difference—not talk about it, not lay claim to it, but to actually see a real difference. In some ways, I think women use their power more subtly than men and without the fanfare. My son once told me that you don't have power if you don't use it—so I've tried to push myself to be more aggressive. I've learned to make tough decisions and stick to them.

Our Secret Weapon: Multitasking

Women multitask a lot better than men. I like to joke that we can get a lot more done in a short period of time. We load the laundry. We pick up the kids. We go to the grocery store. Then we do our homework, our reading. The guys? Half the time, they just have to show up for meetings.

Don't Burn Bridges

Don't burn bridges—it's not worth it. Rather than saying, "I want to achieve this goal—and by the way, you're an idiot because you don't agree with me," remember that everybody in the room basically wants to arrive at the same place. There will be small arguments and large arguments, but I've found that regardless of one's political philosophy or party, we all want the same things. We want a prosperous and safe country where everybody's

treated equally, with the liberties and freedoms our forefathers fought for.

Sometimes It's the Little Things

When I was first sworn in, my father, as a former member
of Congress, was able to join me on the House floor. You
can imagine how proud we were. The day went pretty
slowly because we were doing a roll call, and I asked my
dad, "Do you remember where the ladies room is around
here?"

He said, "Honey, when I was in Congress there were
only three of you, and you had to knock at the men's room
to get in."

Now, of course, congresswomen have their own lounge,
and on the wall is a portrait of Jeannette Rankin of
Montana—the first woman elected to Congress, before
women even had the right to vote.

How We Protect the Ones Protecting Us

In the women's caucus, we have real opportunities for bipartisan progress on a range of issues that affect women
today. Partisanship really isn't a factor, and we seek common ground. When I was chairman of the caucus, we focused on addressing sexual assault in the military.

We ask our servicemen and -women to go into very
difficult situations in foreign lands, and with women
serving in greater numbers than ever before, we felt
that the protocols surrounding sexual assault just hadn't

caught up. Unfortunately in Iraq and in Afghanistan we were finding that some women in the military were being sexually assaulted by their colleagues. This posed a real challenge, not only for our military women but also for the continuity of our entire force. So we went to the Department of Defense and asked them to do a study, to set up protocols to ensure that military women had access to resources like sexual assault centers that are available in civilian life. We meet annually to monitor progress and make sure we're moving in the right direction.

___

My words for young women

I'm proud that women have a louder voice than in the past—but we need to make that voice even louder.

___

Speaking Out Without Fear

Madeleine Kunin

First woman governor of Vermont (D) · First woman to serve
three terms as governor of any state · Former U.S.
ambassador to Switzerland

Seventy-six Male Governors in a Row, and Then—Me

In 1984, when I walked into the executive office of the
Vermont State House after the election, I scanned the row
of portraits of somber male governors with names like
Ebenezer and Erastus. They stared down as if to say,
"What are *you* doing here?" In 2006, when nine-year-old
Melissa Campbell visited that beautiful state house and
came upon my portrait, she exclaimed, "Finally, a woman.
It's about time."

This is where we are today: We believe it's about time
for women to be involved in every level of government.
Nancy Pelosi is Speaker of the House, third in line of suc-
cession to the presidency. When she is seen on television
wielding the gavel, she sends young women a message
that they belong there.

Women hold 17 percent of the seats in the U.S. Congress, and that's an all-time high. It is also about average in parliaments around the world, so you might say, well, that's not so bad. But in a list put out by the United Nations, the United States ranks seventy-second out of 142 countries. Iraq and Afghanistan have more women in their parliaments than we do.

Words I live by

"Failure is impossible."
—Susan B. Anthony

Why Don't I Get a Seat at the Table?

I first ran for the Vermont legislature in the 1970s, and one of that decade's revolutions, the women's movement, gave me permission to combine my two goals—to have both a family and a career. The woman's movement also gave me an issue: the Equal Rights Amendment, which was proposed as a constitutional amendment but never ratified. It simply stated that there shall be no discrimination on the basis of sex. I lobbied the Vermont legislature as a private citizen for that amendment. As I spoke to legislators I began to think, *Instead of knocking on the doors of power and pleading to come in, why don't I get a seat at the table?*

On a deeper level, I think I was also influenced by my autobiography. I came to the United States from Switzerland as a child and couldn't speak English. My mother said to me and my brother what all immigrant parents tell their children: "Anything is possible in America." We believed this. It gave us a sense of optimism. And optimism is a very important criterion for entering public life.

My family came to the United States in 1940 because of World War II. It was a time when Hitler was occupying much of Europe. The Holocaust was very close to my experience; I lost aunts and uncles and cousins. At some point in my life I realized I was very privileged because I survived. I could speak out without fear as a Jewish woman, something my parents and grandparents could not do. I felt I should use this opportunity to speak out whenever I could. This feeling formed the bedrock of my sense of social concern, which translated into running for office.

Our Secret Weapon: Anger

What makes you risk stepping into the public arena? First, I think you have to have a certain level of anger. You may be provoked by something small, like a problem in your neighborhood, or something big, like global warming. For me, it was concern about my children walking to school and having to cross a dangerous railroad track. I was angry enough to act and figure out what had to be done. But if you're too angry about an issue, it doesn't work. You can either say, "Nothing's going to happen, why take the risk?

Wake me up in twenty years and tell me what happened," or "The system doesn't work, burn the place down; I'll become a revolutionary." That's happening in many parts of the world where people take to the streets and turn to terrorism.

But if you're just angry enough, you move into the second phase, where you engage your imagination. You allow yourself to imagine a world that is somewhat different from what exists today. And it can be something small, like a flashing red light at a railroad crossing. You don't have to have the complete answer; you just have to have a vision, an idea. Then you move to the third phase, where you find your optimism. There's a saying that pessimists are usually right, but optimists change the world.

In the 2008 presidential election, something unusual happened. There was a level of anger and a flowering of imagination about the future. In past elections, when people got excited about a candidate, it was the young men who came home after the campaign and decided to run for office. This time Barack Obama and Hillary Clinton, in a different way, inspired a new generation of voters. My hope in this is that after this election, an equal number of young women and young men will continue to carry the torch to run for office. Because in this election, women were not relegated to making coffee, as we once were. We were involved at every level of the campaign.

Women change the conversation when they are in the room. We need your experiences not only to represent yourself, but to represent all those people who can't be at the table. Politics can be nasty, you know that. But politics is where change happens. And it's been the most exciting part of my life. I haven't succeeded in everything I've wanted to do, but I've had that glorious feeling of having succeeded from time to time. It is better to live life in the rushing stream with all its rocks and dangers than to sit by the side of the stream and watch life go by. And you are the generation we need. You will be the ones who can change your communities, your states, your country, and the world.

Finding Your Own Voice

When women rise to the top, they're caught in a double bind. They have to be tough enough for the job, but they also have to be feminine and likeable. We saw a case study of this in Hillary Clinton's campaign. She met the toughness test right off. But there was a lot of questioning about whether she was likeable and feminine enough. It's hard for women in top leadership positions because we've all grown up in a culture of predominantly male leadership, and we still tend to judge women by these models.

Don't let that stop you. Running for office means using your voice. To stand in the public eye, you don't have to conform to a political stereotype. What you really have to do is find your own voice and trust your own beliefs. That's probably the hardest part. Once you step out of your comfort zone, there are strangers listening to what you say. You could be attacked, criticized. But if you care passionately about something, you will be able to do it. Don't be afraid of dissent and debate—enjoy it.

Don't Wait to Be Asked

Don't underestimate your own abilities, which is something women often do. Your experiences may be different from those of a man, but they are equally important. If you've volunteered in the schools or organized a fund drive for an organization, you've learned about education and fund-raising at the grassroots level. Those are important qualifications for public life. Women, more than men, need to be asked to run. Don't wait to be asked. It's not unfeminine or arrogant to put yourself out there and say, "I can represent you, I can help you, and I'm qualified to do this job."

Why We Need Women in Charge

As governor, I governed like the men before me about 90 to 95 percent of the time. But that 5 to 10 percent made a difference. I put more money in the budget for subsidized child care, because as a mother I knew how important child care was for working women, particularly low-income women. It could make the difference between being able to support their families or not. We funded rape crisis centers and battered women's shelters because I knew how women's lives were affected by these forms of assistance. We started a children's health insurance program called Dr. Dynasaur. All these initiatives were related to my experiences as a woman.

Be Under the Influence—of Women

I didn't know I would become a politician until I was in my thirties. Then I was strongly influenced by the women's movement and figures such as Betty Friedan, Gloria Steinem, Bella Abzug, and others. Earlier, my role model was Eleanor Roosevelt.

MY IDEA OF POWER DRESSING

You don't need a power suit, just an outfit that's not controversial and will not take away from what you are saying. I think the simple answer is to dress well, be comfortable, and enjoy what you're wearing.

My words for young women

The reason to seek power is to empower others. That is what power means in politics.

A Process Tailor-Made for Women's Strengths

Lisa Maatz

Director, public policy and government relations for the
American Association of University Women (AAUW)

The Great Grammar School Bathroom Door Revolt

I'm a lobbyist, but I use my powers for good.

I know we don't have the best reputation these days.
But nonprofit, do-gooder lobbyists like me are a far cry
from the Gucci Gulch power brokers on K Street. I work
for the American Association of University Women, a national organization that works to break through educational and economic barriers so all women have a fair
chance. Every day, through the actions of this powerful
network of educated women and men, I am reminded of
the importance of grassroots advocacy. I have enormous
respect for the power of collective voices to make social
change, and I learned this respect the old-fashioned way.

I grew up in a small town just outside Cleveland, Ohio.
In the 1970s Hinckley was a lot like other Rust Belt towns:
filled with hardworking people going through tough times.

I attended an elementary school with dedicated teachers but few resources. Our social studies book was so behind the times it didn't reflect the fact that a man had landed on the moon. These neglected facilities set the stage for my first lesson in grassroots organizing.

I was eight years old. At Hinckley Elementary School, the doors to the stalls in the girls' restroom had fallen off and never been replaced. We'd go to the restroom in groups, with one girl doing her business while the rest of us stood facing outward, blocking the stall and providing the privacy we craved. We didn't think much about it until we heard that the boys had doors in *their* restroom. I remember thinking, quite practically, that the girls would use the doors a lot more and it seemed only fair that we have them too. Simple third-grade logic.

I was pals with the principal, and I was sure if I told him about this predicament he'd take care of it. So I went to Mr. Ginke—probably the best elementary school principal name on the planet—and told him about my door dilemma. I made sure he understood that the boys had doors, and asked if the girls could have doors too. Mr. Ginke was the school's all-powerful problem solver, and nice to boot. I figured, no sweat—he'd sympathize and take care of things like he always did.

Imagine my surprise when Mr. Ginke literally patted me on the head and told me not to worry about it. End of conversation. The exchange left a bad taste in my mouth, and I went home disappointed not only that Mr. Ginke had denied my request, but also that he didn't seem to understand why it was important to me.

I didn't know precisely why I felt out of sorts, I just knew I wanted to do something about it. But what? I worried about it all weekend. That Monday at school, I made my move. I started a petition asking for new doors in the girls' restroom. As you can imagine, this caused a stir. It took some work to get the first few of my friends to sign—they didn't want to get in trouble—but in a few days we had almost all the third- and fourth-grade girls on board and even some of the boys. By then it had become cool to sign the petition.

At the end of the week, my moment of truth arrived. It was time to deliver the petition to Mr. Ginke. I remember the trepidation I felt when I walked into his office, put my petition on his desk, and said very clearly, "Mr. Ginke, I'm not the only one who wants doors."

That's all I said. Mr. Ginke looked kind of stunned. I remember him reading the petition, this little-girl petition, on ragged-edged paper ripped from a spiral notebook, with lopsided hearts drawn in pink Magic Marker. Then he smiled. As much as my persistence frustrated him, I think he was a bit tickled too.

A week later, we had our doors. They weren't great doors, just rough plywood, painted slate blue and mounted on the squeakiest of hinges. But they were music to my ears. Remember, I had first asked for doors all by myself and got nothing. In fact, I got worse than nothing—I got dismissed, even disrespected. But when I gave Mr. Ginke a petition signed by two hundred of my classmates, I had doors in a week. Just think how such a lesson could shape your sense of the world at the age of eight.

Words I live by

"The truth will set you free.
But first, it will piss you off."
—GLORIA STEINEM

I've posted this feminist take on the oft-quoted biblical passage beside my desk. To me, it speaks to the fact that knowledge is power, and the emotions spurred by that knowledge—anger, disbelief, determination—can fruitfully be used to change the status quo.

Who Has the Power? You Do.

In a way, that's what the AAUW is all about: the power of voices united to command both change and respect. It's 100,000 women working on issues we care about, on Title 9 and pay equity, on economic security, retirement security, access to education for women and girls. Yes, I represent our members on Capitol Hill. But I am only as strong as our AAUW grassroots network. At the end of the day, it's my members who hold their elected officials accountable—in letters and op-eds, at town hall meetings, and ultimately at the ballot box. It's that accountability that gives me the power to make my case.

Because of my background (an undergraduate degree in political science and sociology; master's degrees in women's studies and journalism; a stint as director of a battered women's shelter) I came to Washington, D.C., armed with respect for the political process. I understand the issues. I know how Congress works. But unless I can actually tell members of Congress I've got constituents at home who are paying attention, I can't have the impact I want, no matter how persuasive or articulate I am. That is the power of the people in a representative democracy, and that's why it's so critical that citizens speak their minds to their elected officials. The AAUW doesn't have a political action committee. We don't give political contributions or endorse candidates. For the AAUW it's all about collectively speaking truth to power in the most organized, effective way possible. It's about grassroots advocacy. Never doubt that it has the power to make the world a better place.

Know Your Line in the Sand

Know your line in the sand, because politics is rarely black and white. It's easy to get lost in shades of gray if you don't have a firm set of personal standards and stick to them. If you do, you'll not only be able to make the tough choices, but you'll also be able to look at yourself in the mirror each morning.

Power, One Small Bite at a Time

I still believe that one person can make a difference— I've seen it happen. But I'm also well aware of the limitations, obstacles, and brick walls along the way. Working inside the reality-free zone of the Washington Beltway, I've become what I call a pragmatic idealist: I work toward big goals incrementally, taking one strategic bite of the apple at a time and using the sweet taste of those victories to fuel the next fight. Our system of government limits the possibility for quick, sweeping change, but that's also the genius of it. The key is to not give up in frustration in the face of slow progress, but to learn how to make the system work for you—and relish the challenge.

Do Women Wield Power Differently?

Sometimes, sometimes not. But I do believe that women are more likely to put it all on the line, to fall on their swords when it really matters to them—and that selfless conviction can save the day when it comes to making social change.

Small, Simple Ways to Change the World

Be a good citizen advocate: Write a letter to the editor, request a meeting with your legislators, stand up at a town meeting, or call your representative's office. *You don't have to be an expert. You simply need to be passionate about the issues. And you need to have an opinion about what might solve the problem at hand.* Don't let the trappings of office intimidate you or prevent you from speaking your mind. A strong democracy is fueled by citizens willing to ask questions, demand answers, and seek change.

The political process is tailor-made for women's strengths—our ability to communicate persuasively and stubbornly persist until things improve. Women running for office often feel they need training and leadership programs before they take the leap. But men seem to feel immediately entitled and qualified, no matter what their experience. Why is that? If you know a woman who'd make a good elected official, tell her. Ask her to run. Let her know you believe in her—you might be surprised at the result.

Who'll Get More Women into Office? You Will.

We now have the first woman speaker of the house, two steps removed from the presidency. We have more women as power committee chairs in the House and Senate than ever before, including the first ever Senate committee led by both a woman committee chair and a woman ranking member. And we had the first woman credibly vie for the presidency—and oh, by the way, she is now the secretary of state, the third woman to hold the job since that particular glass ceiling was broken just over a decade ago. That's pretty powerful stuff. At the same time, there are fewer than eighty women in the House and only seventeen in the Senate, and only a handful of women in governorships nationwide. So, yes, we're making progress, but it's slow and arduous. I think Nancy Pelosi's ascension and

Hillary Clinton's run for the White House are positive harbingers of things to come, not just in paving the way for more women candidates, but in more women and girls simply imagining the possibilities when they see themselves in their leaders. Images are powerful, and the more women we have in powerful roles, political or not, the more girls will follow in their footsteps.

Sometimes You Just Have to Keep Going

My mom is my role model and my inspiration. A gifted nurse with three kids, always a working mom, she still found the time to do community work. She ran the PTA and founded the women's club. Before my parents' divorce, she was a political wife too, married to a town council member who was also president of the local chamber of commerce, and she wielded that power for causes she believed in. She headed committees and fund-raisers, started petitions, and wrote letters to the editor. For Mom, it has always been about making things better for her kids. She is still an avid newspaper reader, news watcher, and public commenter on political and community affairs, despite troubling health issues that keep her home much of the time. I once asked her how she stayed so optimistic despite the hurdles, and she said, "I kept going because sometimes you just have to keep going." Truly, I did not come to this calling by accident.

My words for young women

Never burn a bridge if you can help it. Washington, D.C., is a company town, and the sphere of politics is amazingly small. Yesterday's intern is today's Capitol Hill legislative director and tomorrow's White House adviser. Relationships are central to getting political work done—who you know and what they know about you.

Which leads me to the next piece: Keep your word. Once you make a promise, deliver the goods. Share the credit when appropriate, and always thank people: Nothing ever gets done in a vacuum, and political people have very long memories.

Powerful Beyond Measure

Michelle Bernard

President and CEO, Independent Women's Forum ·
Political and legal analyst, MSNBC · Columnist, *The
Washington Examiner* · Author, *Women's Progress*

Fear No Man

My secret is simple: When I was a child, my parents always told me to "fear no man." They meant that there was no one—black or white, male or female—who was "more equal" than any of us. My siblings and I were taught that with education and hard work, there was nothing we could not achieve, and that we should always strive to be the best.

My parents emigrated from Jamaica to attend undergraduate and graduate school in Washington, D.C., where I was born. I grew up hearing the motto of my father's high school: "The Utmost for the Highest." It's ironic that this motto comes from an all-male school, Calabar High School, which has graduated some of Jamaica's greatest leaders. My sisters and I were taught this refrain even though Jamaica is a very macho, male-oriented society. The conventional wisdom in our culture was that boys were raised to be leaders, and girls, though given an education, were raised to be good wives. I remember watching a female politician giving a speech on television and one of my uncles proclaiming, "That woman could never have a husband!"

Despite this, my parents made a concerted effort to raise my sisters and me no differently than they raised my brother. My siblings and I were incredibly competitive. We played sports and played to win. When my sister enrolled in a high school that did not have a girls' tennis team, my parents signed her up for the boys' team. I raced against boys when I was on my high school track team as a way to hone my skills and get even faster. We grew up loving politics. We learned to debate and participated in student government.

Words I live by

Our deepest fear is not that we are inadequate.
Our deepest fear is that we are powerful
  beyond measure.

—MARIANNE WILLIAMSON,
from *A Return to Love*

Make Your Job Fit Your Life, Not Vice Versa

I began my career practicing law, a common entry point to politics and policy. But legal work did not offer me the deeper satisfaction I wanted and became increasingly incompatible with my desire to begin a family. I joined the Independent Women's Forum—a nonprofit organization that focuses on policy issues related to women's rights—to help advance democracy and women's rights in the Middle East, but also because it was a job that would leave me more time for parenting. The joke was on me, because the hours are almost as bad as they were at my law firm, and for a lot less pay. But I do have more flexibility now—and I love what I do.

All Issues Are Women's Issues

Now, as president of the organization, I speak out on issues and promote the work of IWF's scholars. IWF's mantra is that *all* issues are women's issues. We believe it limits women's impact when they are pigeonholed as being interested only in a subset of policy debates— reproductive rights, for example. IWF scholars speak on just about all domestic and foreign policy issues: war, economic recovery, terrorism, health care, education, Social Security, and government spending.

IWF also provides a forum for arguments and ideologies often ignored by more left-of-center women's organizations. There are people who assume that because I am a woman or because I am black, I am an advocate of big-government solutions to society's problems. But we are all individuals first, and I believe in the free market and a limited role for government. When I started my career, it was largely assumed that all women involved in politics were pro-choice and Democratic. That's changed. Today, many self-identified feminists are pro-life, free-market Republicans.

Supporting Women Candidates of All Stripes

When I graduated from law school, the most prominent national group focused on electing women was EMILY's List (an acronym for Early Money Is Like Yeast). Its mission is to recruit and promote pro-choice Democratic women to government. Within a few short years, we witnessed the development of an organization called The WISH List (Women In the Senate and House). Its focus is to identify, train, and support pro-choice Republican women candidates. After 1992, there was also the Susan B. Anthony List, which is dedicated to supporting pro-life female candidates. The existence of such organizations, along with the presidential and vice presidential campaigns of Hillary Clinton and Sarah Palin, demonstrate the diversity of women in politics now.

Our mission at IWF is to advance economic liberty, personal responsibility, and political freedom. These are important values for all people, women and men. We are committed to ensuring that women's voices are heard on all policy issues. It's a lot of work, but it's the best job I have ever had. It has allowed me to find my voice—and to help other women and men find theirs.

Continuing an American Tradition

I became involved with politics and policy as a result of a strong desire to make a difference in the lives of those who are invisible—to hear the voices of those who are rarely sought out and listened to in a world where politics and policy intersect.

In college I studied the writings of John Locke and Thomas Jefferson. I have always thought that our nation's Declaration of Independence is the greatest document ever written. The phrase "We hold these truths to be self-evident, that all men are created equal, that they are endowed by their Creator with certain unalienable Rights, that among these are Life, Liberty, and the pursuit of Happiness" has been the most powerful tool in our nation's history in abolishing slavery and advancing the rights of African-Americans and women. I joined the Independent Women's Forum because it is an organization that would allow me to advance and promote these ideals.

My goals did not change after I acquired political experience. What did change was the way I viewed the world. I started out with a very innocent view about how government worked. I was wrong: There is no room for naïveté in politics, and commitment is not enough. One must be strategic in the pursuit of a goal. Additionally, I learned that one must be able to see both sides of an issue, and have a lot of patience and fortitude. Most important, one must have an incorruptible sense of right and wrong and strength of character, even while recognizing that not everyone shares these values.

Don't Be the One to Limit Yourself

The most valuable secret I would share with young women about seeking a successful career in politics: Know that it can happen at any time in your life. Whether you're straight out of college, a high school student, a dropout, a stay-at-home mom, a single mother, or even a retiree, you can enter politics successfully. We stand on the shoulders of many great women. Some were escaped slaves; many were uneducated and impoverished; others were wealthy and powerful. All these women prove that no matter your circumstance, you can make a difference in the political arena, and your words and actions matter. Women can seek out the highest office of the land if they so desire. The only thing that limits us is our ability to dream.

Steer Clear of Stereotypes

Don't let yourself be typecast ideologically or locked into the stereotypical politics of "women's issues." Women are not single-issue voters; nor are they a monolithic voting bloc. Women are affected by the same issues as men. While questions of reproductive rights, domestic violence, or sexual harassment in the workplace have unique relevance to women, we're also affected by the ongoing economic crisis, education and health care reform, energy policy, national security and terrorism, and the many other serious issues we now face. Young women entering politics should expect—and should make clear to those around them that they expect—to sit at the power table when all issues and political ideologies are debated.

A Woman Will Become President

When I began my career, a female governor or senator was almost a rarity. Now they are commonplace. Today, it would be bizarre not to see several women among any gathering of top political officials. Equally important, there no longer is a sense that women are limited to certain jobs—those involving social services and domestic policy, for instance. In recent years, women have dominated the position of secretary of state. They have served as national security adviser and United Nations ambassador. Female legislators serve on the armed services, intelligence, and foreign relations committees. There are an increasing number of female general officers in the military. In time, women will head the CIA and the U.S. Department of Defense—and occupy the Oval Office.

Another change: Women used to obtain political power by starting at the local level (i.e., being elected to the local school board), working their way up to elected office at the state level, and then maybe running for the U.S. Congress. Much of women's political power was focused on influencing local communities and their families. Today, there are many avenues for women to gain political power on a broader scale. It's not uncommon to see women run for state or national office or be appointed to a cabinet-level position without any prior experience in politics.

There Is Nothing We Cannot Achieve

My mother is the greatest and most powerful woman I have ever known. She emigrated to the United States as a college freshman to attend Howard University in Washington, D.C. While still a student, she married my father. She gave birth to four children, finished college and graduate school, and raised all of us with a love that is impossible to describe as anything other than pure bliss. She has taught each of us to love God and love one another, to treasure family, to treasure and enjoy every moment of our lives with our own children, to love education and be lifelong learners, and to know that there is nothing we cannot achieve.

As a very young child, I had a homework assignment to color in some pictures. I am black, and everyone I knew was black, so I colored all the people brown. My teacher objected, but I refused to color the people in my coloring book any other color. I was reprimanded, and my parents were called in. I'll always remember my mother telling me that all was well—to always stand up for myself and what I believe in, and to remember that as a black girl, I, too, was beautiful.

When I was eighteen, my mother wrote the following in a Bible she gave me: "Please read this Bible always. When you are happy, when you are sick, when you are despondent, and when you are lonely, always know that God loves you as do your mother and father. Have faith, be unselfish, your Godliness will shine through." These words have stayed with me and greatly influenced my life.

The Power to Say No

The first time I ever felt political power enabled me to achieve something great was when I was chairman of the District of Columbia's Redevelopment Agency (RLA board), whose mission is to "eliminate the dilapidated and blighted areas of the city through rehabilitation, clearance, and redevelopment." When I joined the RLA board, I never could have foreseen my involvement in one of the most significant real estate development projects in the District of Columbia at the time, the development of the MCI Center (now called the Verizon Center). Nor did I foresee that as a young professional, with little if any political experience, I would publicly butt heads with the mayor of the District of Columbia and oppose many members of the district's political and economic machinery.

This was an enormous political battle, and I survived it. Mayor Marion Barry and many members of the city council thought that the city should pay all the costs for the new arena. I remember thinking that D.C. government had just cut $33 million from the school budget of one of the poorest-performing school districts in the country, and some genius thought that a better way to spend the taxpayers' money was to build a sports arena. So as chairman of the RLA board, I said no. I questioned whether this proposed expenditure was the proper role of government, and demanded—and got—a public-private partnership to finance the development. Later, Mayor Barry wanted the district to take out loans from private lenders to pay its share of the costs. I thought this proposition too expensive and said no. My colleagues and I went to Wall Street and were able to execute a bond deal to finance the district's portion of the development costs. By some estimates, our deal saved district residents millions of dollars. Today, this once blighted area is alive with banks, restaurants, retail, and other businesses that bring jobs and revenue to the district every year.

POWER DRESSING

I love simple, elegant, and feminine clothing, especially dresses and pantsuits. However, it is not the clothing that makes me feel powerful; I feel powerful just by virtue of the fact that I am a woman and a mother. I think the scrutiny of women's clothing choices is asinine.

My words for young women

Your goal should be to live life to the fullest, make the most of your opportunities, and help fully realize humankind's natural right to freedom, peace, and equality under the law.

Whatever It Is That Moves You . . . Embrace It

Leticia Van de Putte

State senator (D), 26th district of Texas · Co-chair, 2008
Democratic National Convention · Member, National
Hispanic Caucus of State Legislators

What My Grandmothers Taught Me

My journey to power began long before I was born. It began with my grandmothers, one of whom was born in Guadalajara, Mexico, and the other in Múzquiz, Coahuila, in a border state in a land we call "La Frontera." Although my grandmothers were only able to attend school until third grade, they were very bright and wonderful women who were the leaders of our family. My maternal grandmother, "Memo," was a great businesswoman and wrote beautiful poetry. She set an example for my mom and really impressed upon her the importance of education. My mother was the first in her family to graduate from college. I am continually amazed at my mother's persistence, as she went to college part time for almost sixteen years.

I start with their stories because their stories are inextricably linked with my own. No one achieves anything alone; we are all building upon a legacy left by someone else: a family member, a teacher, a neighbor, or a pastor— people who inspired us or helped us take the next step or meet the next challenge.

The first generations of working women were teachers, nurses, social workers, and secretaries. They were true pioneers to open those doors, because before them no one had thought that women should work outside the home. Then came my generation, which had more opportunity to have a professional life, but only when someone really advocated for us. Discrimination against women was embedded in our fundamental institutions: public schools, churches, and, of course, the workplace.

Words I live by

"My faith in the Constitution is whole,
it is complete, and it is total. I am not going
to sit here and be an idle spectator to the
diminution, the subversion, the destruction
of the Constitution."

—TEXAS CONGRESSWOMAN
BARBARA JORDAN

I remember when I was in the eighth grade, watching Barbara Jordan on TV during the Watergate hearings and hearing her say these words. I was mesmerized. I thought, *How can a woman, particularly a woman of color, be so powerful and articulate?* She was in a room full of powerful and elite white men, but they were all listening to her ask the tough questions. I wanted to be like her, to demand accountability from our leaders and to speak with conviction and authority. Her allure was not based on her physical beauty, but on her brilliant mind, forceful voice, and unquestionable logic.

Years later, as a first-term House member, when then-governor Ann Richards asked if there was anything she could do for me, I replied, "I want to meet Barbara Jordan." A few weeks later Governor Richards invited me to a casual dinner party at the governor's mansion. When I arrived, the dinner party consisted of me, Governor Richards, the irrepressible Liz Carpenter, and Barbara Jordan. We talked long into the early morning, and the congresswoman extended an invitation for me to join her summer program at the Lyndon Baines Johnson School at the University of Texas, which groomed local and state female politicians for higher public office. Meeting Barbara Jordan was a real turning point for me. She was someone who had not only obtained political power, but had also changed traditional thinking about women of color.

Challenging the Built-in Bias

I wanted to be a pharmacist because my grandfather was a pharmacist. He ran an old-time Mexican pharmacy, La

Botica Guadalupana, in downtown San Antonio. He was held in high esteem by our community because he helped people. I wanted people to respect me the way they respected him.

When I was in ninth grade, the math class for girls was home economics, because, it was argued, women used fractions in cooking and needed to learn how to write checks and balance the family budget. But if a girl wanted to be a doctor, pharmacist, dentist, architect, or engineer, she had to take algebra in ninth grade, because any pre-med, science, or engineering major in college required four years of math, including both algebra and calculus. That's why those fields were traditionally male dominated, because there was a systematic elimination of women. I knew I wanted to be a pharmacist, and I was lucky enough to have parents who challenged the administration and insisted I be allowed to take algebra.

My work as a pharmacist is what actually led to me into public office. In the 1980s we had a mandatory policy in Texas whereby every cow was required to have full vaccinations, and it was recorded in a registry. Inexplicably, we did not have a similar policy for children. As a pharmacist, I knew the importance of preventive care, and I thought to myself, *Who's making these rules? What sense does it make to spend hundreds of thousands of dollars on a premature infant, but not spend a lousy $1.39 a month for prenatal vitamins to ensure a healthy birth in the first place?* So my advocacy came more from anger than anything else. There was a vacancy in the legislature and I put my name in. I wasn't supposed to win. The candidates were five men and me, but there was a group of women and friends who supported me and I won. I have loved public policy ever since.

Fight for What You Love

My secret to power is passion: Use your background or whatever issues are important to you as the catalyst to public office. For some, it might be the environment and the fact that we're not being good stewards of this beautiful earth God has given us, and a fear that it won't be here for the next generation. For others, it might be making sure that every child, regardless of last name or birthplace, has access to quality education. There are so many causes that need champions and so many voiceless people who need a voice.

This generation of young people had a real awakening with the 2008 presidential election. I have not seen young people so engaged in their government since my generation's protests of the Vietnam War. Maybe it was because Barack Obama connected with young people in a way I haven't seen in a very, very long time. I am optimistic because this generation has so much to give. This generation is technology savvy and they embrace new challenges without fear. Whatever it is that they choose to engage in must originate from their hearts, and it's got to be for the right reasons. I hope our young leaders will transfer their energy from the presidential election to other challenges facing their communities, and then encourage other young people to join their cause.

The Future Is Up to Us

My grandmother was very, very wise and she always used these little *dichos*—little Mexican bits of wisdom. One of her favorites was *Si sabe lo que no sabes, sabes algo,* which means, "If you know what you don't know, you know something." We live in a complex world. We don't know what the future holds, but as people of faith we know who holds the future. We know that if we don't invest in our country, our young people, and their education, and if we don't invest in our infrastructure—not just roads and bridges but in our people, our human capital— then we are not going to remain a country we can all be proud of. The next generation will wonder what the hell we were all doing and why we weren't working as hard as we could to secure their future.

Our founding fathers were working for all of us over 200 years ago when they drafted our Constitution. They wanted a better and more secure future for the next generation. That is the greatness of America: our desire to repair our faults and to work continually toward a brighter future. One day, women like Hillary Clinton and Michelle Obama will no longer be the exception but the norm. We will be everywhere, in public office, leading nonprofits, running Fortune 500 companies and small businesses. By following our passions, we can become an army of powerful and passionate women working to bring positive change to our nation.

Every Child Deserves an Opportunity

When I first ran for the Texas House, I was motivated by a desire to help our very young children receive quality health care and a great education. I also wanted to make a difference for small businesses, especially because of the increasing entrepreneurship of women. I still care greatly about our youth, but I am also more focused on economic empowerment and opportunity for families. Each child should have the opportunity to attend great neighborhood schools, graduate, and be ready for postsecondary training. Having those opportunities will provide a strong foundation for any community and increase a family's earning power.

I believe in the Declaration of Independence's assertion that "All men are created equal." But those words lack meaning when the quality of education is determined by where you live or who your parents are.

Be Confident, Not Boastful

Whatever moves you, embrace it, be proud of it. Then engage! Learn with your mind and lead with your heart. If you are passionate, all the other stuff will just fall into place.

Be confident, but not boastful. It is not always about you, it's about the entire team. Try and suppress the desire for total control. A strong leader will capitalize on and strengthen her teammates' leadership abilities. Your teammates can do a great job if you allow them to, so empower them. Realize that everyone, even you, will make mistakes, but a great leader acknowledges a mistake, learns from it, and moves on.

Always remember the primary purpose of an elected official should be to bring public value, not personal pleasure—and hopefully, you will get intense personal pleasure from adding public value. If it's only about the power, you will never truly be fulfilled.

Leave the School Cafeteria Behind

Avoid gossip. Remember to deal in truth, not hearsay; stick to the issues at hand, not personalities. This is not the high school prom, this is real life—and the stakes are high.

Worthy Sacrifices

The first women legislators in Texas were in office because someone gave it to them. They occupied seats once held by a father or husband, and when he died, they were sent to Austin as a replacement.

Fortunately, today's young women are not defined by who their daddies or husbands are. Now, many women policymakers arise out of community activist backgrounds. These women choose an issue of utmost importance to them and build their own networks.

There is still a bias against women in politics. Some people think that parenting and politics are mutually exclusive, and that you can't be a good mother if you're gone so often. Our families do make sacrifices, but the sense of accomplishment and satisfaction of knowing that your efforts have helped other children make it worthwhile.

In my second legislative session as a House member, I was able to secure a $200 million appropriation for the Children's Cancer Institute in San Antonio. I was present for the groundbreaking and took my son with me so he could see what had kept his mom away from him. It was really important to me that my little boy see that his mom had played a key role in building a program and research center to help sick boys and girls.

POWER DRESSING

To be taken seriously, you have to dress seriously. I love a sexy dress as much as the next girl, but there is a time and a place for everything. My power accessories are high heels and lipstick. High heels allow me to feel feminine and in command—and besides, they are awfully sexy. "Give me my lipstick!" is my battle cry for going into tough negotiations or prolonged floor debates.

Take Up Golf If You Have To

Beth Frerking

Assistant managing editor, Partnerships at POLITICO ·
Journalist for 30 years · On reporting team that became
a Pulitzer Prize finalist for its series on air traffic safety

Feminism Is Not a Dirty Word

When I was a college student in the late 1970s, being a feminist was considered a plus. We wanted to be considered equals to men, yet also be valued for bringing new perspectives to the workplace. We saw ourselves as pioneers, even as we appreciated the women who broke ground for us. So it came as quite a surprise when I recently discovered that many young women consider feminism an archaic, even annoying concept. For them, it brings to mind stridency and humorlessness, bra burning and overly earnest consciousness-raising rap sessions. Forget about the profound political and cultural ideals it incorporates and celebrates. Many younger women say they're simply beyond feminism and prefer not to categorize themselves so narrowly. Rather, they want to be seen, included, and judged as individuals with good ideas and contributions to make, not only as women (or African-Americans or Latinas or whatever).

They may need to do a reality check, especially with their male peers. Younger men may be more progressive and open-minded about women's abilities than their fathers, but many still take their cues from the people in charge. And those people tend to be older men who still view women, consciously or not, as not quite equal to the task, especially in the heat of competition.

Take some of the criticisms of former Alaska governor Sarah Palin when Senator John McCain chose her as his running mate in the 2008 presidential election. Put aside political ideology and look at the way she was questioned for running when she had a new baby, especially one with Down syndrome. You heard it again and again: "How dare she go back to work so soon after having a baby!" I was astonished and disturbed by the ferocity of those attacks.

Here's the rub: This is simply not a question that would have been raised had Sarah Palin been Sam Palin—a male vice presidential nominee who had just had a child. So our progress isn't complete. We're not there.

Words I live by

"Many women have more power than they recognize, and they're very hesitant to use it, for they fear they won't be loved."
—FORMER COLORADO CONGRESSWOMAN PAT SCHROEDER

It's Important to Be Stealthy

How do we continue to raise consciousness about women and family issues while we succeed in the workplace? Make your mark. I call it stealth. You can get women's issues out there in an in-your-face way. But you're going to be more effective if you learn to play the game. This may sound antifeminist. But when you can meet your colleagues, bosses, and competition knowing your stuff, you will do much better than if you plead special treatment because you're a woman. That's just not going to work.

Can We Have It All?

None of this means, however, that women don't face special challenges if they decide to have children and thrive in their professional lives. I get asked this question whenever I talk to journalism classes: How do you do both?

Well, my two sons never knew me any other way than as a mother who is also a professional journalist. I went back to work after six months off with each of my sons. I was lucky, because I worked for good companies with paid time off. And I had a husband who worked for the federal government and was able to take unpaid paternity leave, thanks in part to a woman representative, Pat Schroeder, who helped push the Family Medical Leave Act through Congress while she was a House member from Colorado.

Whenever the subject of maternity leave arises, we often forget there's an enormous group of mothers for whom staying home is not a option—women in poverty, low- or even middle-income working women who don't have that luxury, even with an employed husband or partner. Don't forget that. Your children will not be scarred for life if you work outside the home. They'll be fine.

Carrying Your Own Message

This brings me back to younger women professionals who are on the cusp of grappling with those kinds of work/family issues. As I listen to them, I sometimes feel disappointed that they don't seem to appreciate the barriers we worked to overcome in the 1970s and early 1980s. But this is how progress works and how we want it to work. They're telling my generation what we told our own parents when we were young: Don't make me carry someone else's message.

I see and hear a strong, positive ethos at work among a younger generation of women reporters, one that I embodied in my early professional career even as I proudly proclaimed the benefits of feminism. It goes like this: I am going to do my job the best I can, and that will get me where I need to get. I am going to study harder, I am going to work harder, and I am not going to make a big deal about being a woman. I am just going to be the best.

There's one more point that shouldn't be lost on all of you who are making your way into your adult lives and careers: Know that you can call on women mentors like us. It makes such a difference when somebody can open a door for you. Don't hesitate to use your connections, because that's something men have never been afraid to do.

You Don't Have to Be Nice

Women are socialized in ways that help us raise families, help us connect and be good negotiators. That's a positive thing, and we should keep and value those skills. But when you are in the workplace, you'll notice that the person who moves up the ladder exudes a confidence that says, "I get to do this because I am the best," and that person is frequently a guy. Don't be afraid to sing your own praises and demand things when you've earned them. Men do it every day with no apologies. Not everybody may end up being your best friend, but don't hesitate. Do it. You'll be a role model for generations of women to come.

My Secret Weapon: Listening

In 1979 I became editor-in-chief of my college newspaper, *The Daily Texan*, when I defeated three male candidates in a campuswide election. I believe I won for two reasons: I was less interested in discussing my political views vis-à-vis the editorial page than in being the steward of a fair, objective, and comprehensive news source, and I campaigned relentlessly. My campaign managers put me before student groups from dawn until late at night, even as I carried a full class load. I met with all kinds of students and listened to their concerns about the newspaper. Since I was running for the only campuswide elected student position at the University of Texas at that time, I felt an obligation to listen to and digest students' concerns. I think they trusted me—and elected me—because of it.

Find the Door to the Back Room

Learn how to play the game. There are still backroom discussions in every profession. I don't happen to think that's a bad thing—as long you know how to get into the back room.

Not all major decisions are made in a convention hall by a popular vote. It doesn't happen that way in politics. It doesn't happen that way in business. I think women in business who take up golf have made one of the best possible decisions. Often, the back room is at the eighteenth green, and they'll be in it.

Avoid the TMI Trap

Don't cry at work. We've seen what happens when politicians cry: If it's a man, he's sensitive; if it's a woman, she's weak. I've done it myself a time or two, but you cry at your peril if you do it in front of your bosses. Just don't. I know this is not always a popular view. We want to accept and accommodate everyone, even if they get emotional. But crying damages you in most workplaces. That is reality.

Also, the American tendency to spill our private lives in public—whether on TV talk shows or in tell-all memoirs—should not extend to the workplace. Heed that little voice in your head that asks, "Is this too much information?"

There Is Still So Much Work to Be Done

I have had very interesting discussions about feminism with some of the younger women reporters at POLITICO and with young women in college. Many of them take women's progress and equality as a given. I think it's a measure of feminists' success that younger women today take it for granted that they'll be judged on their smarts, capabilities, diligence, and creativity, and not just as women. That said, we still don't have enough women in the executive offices and boardrooms, or in higher public office, and I hope younger women will build on the progress we've made.

Rebellion in My Blood

When my maternal grandmother was in high school, she enrolled in a chemistry class, the only girl to do so. The teacher, a man, would never call on her, treating her as if she were invisible. She finally threw her textbook at him to get his attention. She didn't finish college—it was during the Depression and her father, a Methodist preacher, didn't have enough money for her last year's tuition—but she was extremely smart and ran a beer distributorship with my grandfather. She worked when most women of her generation didn't.

My mother went back to college to earn her teaching degree when my sister and I were in elementary school. That meant late nights for her studying, and afternoons when my sister and I arrived home before she did. I was impressed with her intellect and drive, and also with my father's unconditional and enthusiastic support of what she did. He never once questioned that she had the right to do it.

POWER DRESSING

My idea of power dressing? A well-tailored, gorgeous dress suit, stylish, rockin' high heels, and my silver hair. I went silver in my early forties and decided not to color it. I like the way it looks. It says a lot about my self-confidence. I once wrote a column for the online magazine *Slate* about my decision not to dye it and got an outpouring of support from both women and men. But silver hair is not for everyone. (And who knows, I may color my hair some day just for fun!) Women should choose what's best for them personally.

Fair or not, we're scrutinized much more closely than men when it comes to our fashion choices.

My words for young women

Learn to be tough. Confidence grows from hard work. Then you can compete against anyone and everyone. As we say here at POLITICO, welcome to the NFL. Think of yourself—and prepare yourself—as a top draft pick.

Nine winners of Lifetime's Future Frontrunners contest at the
2008 Democratic National Convention in Denver, Colorado

About This Book

Secrets of Powerful Women is a culmination project resulting from Lifetime's fifth Every Woman Counts campaign. First launched in 1992 and executed during each subsequent presidential election cycle, Lifetime's Every Woman Counts campaign is the entertainment industry's only ongoing public advocacy campaign dedicated to amplifying women's voices in the political process, encouraging them to register to vote, speak out on the issues they care about, and run for office.

As part of this campaign, Lifetime hosted the Future Frontrunners contest, designed to spark interest and participation in the political process among high school and college-aged girls. Young women submitted written or video essays explaining what they would do if they were president of the United States. Winners were given the exclusive opportunity to attend the Democratic and Republican national conventions, where they heard firsthand from the many women now featured as contributors in this book.

The hope of this book is to amplify the voices and extend the wisdom of the women leaders in the government, business, and nonprofit sectors who took part in this campaign, so that their words will live indefinitely for the benefit of countless generations to come.

Every Woman Counts Partners & Resources

American Association of University Women (AAUW)	(www.aauw.org)
Business and Professional Women's Foundation	(www.bpwusa.org)
Cancer Schmancer Movement	(www.cancerschmancer.org)
Declare Yourself!	(www.declareyourself.com)
Girls Inc.	(www.girlsinc.org)
Independent Women's Forum	(www.iwf.org)
League of Women Voters	(www.lwv.org)
Lifetime Networks	(www.mylifetime.com)
National Council of Women's Organizations	(www.womensorganizations.org)
National Organization for Women	(www.now.org)
POLITICO	(www.politico.com)
RightNow	(www.rightnow.org)
Girl Scouts of the USA	(www.girlscouts.org)
The White House Project	(www.thewhitehouseproject.org)
The Women's Media Center	(www.womensmediacenter.com)
Voto Latino	(www.votolatino.org)
Women's Voices. Women Vote.	(www.wvwv.org)

These are but a few of the hundreds of national women's groups representing more than 15 million women across the country who have been partners in Lifetime's Every Woman Counts campaigns.

Acknowledgments

I would like to thank the following for their creative ideas, passionate contributions, and hard work on this book: Natalie Byrne, Danielle Carrig, Amanda Crumley, Toby Graff, Geralyn Lucas, Lauren Manzella, and Meredith Wagner of Lifetime Networks, and also Marcia Menter for her editorial skills.

Without their help, the secrets of the powerful women contributors to this book would have, indeed, remained secrets.

—AW

I want to acknowledge several women who've demonstrably guided my journey. I give thanks to my Titi Anna Brown for showing me a woman's strength, Maria Teresa Kumar for being my partner, Eve Ensler for being my mentor, and Jane Fonda and Rita Moreno for being my examples. Last and just as important, I want to give thanks to my namesake, Tia Rosario Alvira, who, in our final conversation, told me that I should never feel like I can't ask God for more.

—RD

In 2007, **Andrea Wong** was named President and CEO of Lifetime Networks, where her creative and business acumen have taken the most powerful women's entertainment brand to new heights. Under her leadership, Lifetime has advanced its mission to celebrate, entertain, and support women through groundbreaking advocacy campaigns that amplify women's voices in their local communities and in Washington's halls of power.

Throughout her career, Wong has demonstrated an unerring ability to identify and anticipate the pulse of American culture. Prior to joining Lifetime, Wong was at ABC, where she was the force behind such pioneering programs as *Dancing with the Stars* and *Extreme Makeover: Home Edition*. Most recently, she spearheaded Lifetime's acquisition of Project Runway, the highest-rated competition show on all of cable.

Wong holds degrees from the Massachusetts Institute of Technology and the Stanford University Graduate School of Business.

Rosario Dawson has garnered praise not only for her numerous leading roles, but also for her work with a range of influential organizations. As an active board member of V-Day, an organization founded by Eve Ensler, she travels worldwide to stop violence against women.

In 2004, Dawson co-founded a nonpartisan political organization called Voto Latino. The group's outreach has targeted youth and helped register over 35,000 voters. Dawson also lends her time and efforts to the Lower Eastside Girls Club in Manhattan and is an ardent environmentalist doing work with a variety of organizations including the Environmental Media Association.

Dawson made her film debut in *Kids* and has since been seen in *Seven Pounds*, *Eagle Eye*, *Sin City*, *Rent*, and *25th Hour*.